PHOEBE

A Journal of Literature and Art

Volume 36   Number 2

Fall 2007

PHOEBE

Fall 2007
Volume 36, Number 2

Editor
Kati Fargo

Assistant Editor
Nat Foster

Fiction Editor
Kelli Ford

Poetry Editor
Shawn Flanagan

Design Editor
Scott Weaver

Assistant Fiction Editor
Ryan Call

Assistant Poetry Editor
Wade Fletcher

Fiction Readers
*Genni Ahrens, Elyse Becker, David Conner,
Regan Douglass, Elizabeth Eshelman, Twila Johnson
Lynnet Ngulube, Laura Thompson*

Poetry Readers
*Edward Davis, Nicole Foreman, Robert Neal St. Lawrence,
Sheri Pappas, Danika Kay Stegeman*

Faculty Advisor
Eric Pankey

Phoebe is a nonprofit literary biannual, edited and produced by students of the MFA program at George Mason University. The editors invite submissions of fiction, poetry, and artwork, which must be postmarked between September 1 and April 15; manuscripts postmarked between April 16 and August 31 will not be read. All manuscripts must be accompanied by a stamped, self-addressed envelope. *Phoebe* does not accept electronic submissions. Complete submission guidelines are on our website: www.gmu.edu/pubs/phoebe

Phoebe is printed by Graphic Communications and indexed by the Index of American Periodical Verse and The American Humanities Index.

The editors would like to thank Michele Braithwaite, Colleen Kearney-Rich, University Publications, and the GMU Creative Writing Program for their support.

Phoebe sponsors annual poetry and fiction contests. The postmark deadline for both contests is December 1. For contest rules, send a stamped, self-addressed envelope, or visit www.gmu.edu/pubs/phoebe

Our subscription rate is $12 for one year (2 issues) or $20 for two years (4 issues). Sample issues are $6. Make checks payable to *Phoebe*.

Phoebe, MSN 2D6
George Mason University
4400 University Drive
Fairfax, VA 22030-4444

www.gmu.edu/pubs/phoebe
phoebe@gmu.edu

Distributed by Bernhard DeBoer, Inc.

ISBN 0-9763484-5-4
© 2007

Table of Contents

——— Special Feature

"The Kangaroo of Ethereal Possibility"
    An Interview with Jonathan Lethem
      & Review of You Don't Love Me Yet
  by Kati Fargo   58

——— Fiction

John Blair	— The Road to Little Happiness	13
Kurtis Davidson	— The Second Coming of Afro-Christ	44
Phong Nguyen	— The Good China	74
M.D. Baumgartner	— Like Gods of the Sun	104

——— Poetry

Angus Bennett	— On Whether the River will Break	6
Eliza Rotterman	— Two Girls	10
Karen Anderson	— Whipping-Bee	11
Martin Corless-Smith	— The 12 to 14 Stations	30
	— Cryptogogic Glossolalia	31
	— [Untitled]	32
	— The Day	34
J. Michael Martinez, James Belflower & Anne Lendon Heide		
	— from Besigned	40
J. Michael Martinez	— Harvest Sun	41
Erin Keane	— The Aerialist Pays a Visit	43

GEORGES GODEAU			
[TRANS BY KATHLEEN MCGOOKEY]			
	—	GRANDMOTHER	56
	—	PERPLEXITY	57
FRED YANNANTUONO	—	AND OUR BRAINS HAVE SAILED AWAY	65
MAYA JEWELL ZELLER	—	THE BOY PRESIDENT	66
JOELLE BIELE	—	TO KATHARINE: AT THREE	67
L.S. KLATT	—	TO WALT WHITMAN IN WINTER	68
	—	ON THE EXCISION OF MAN	69
ELEANOR GRAVES	—	THE AMBIVALENT	70
	—	YOUR BOARDERS	72
JIM GOAR	—	OBEDIENT IS MUM	87
HAINES EASON	—	A SMALL BIRTH THERE	88
	—	HUNT	91
JEANETTE KARHI	—	WORSEN	93
REBA ELLIOTT	—	CHILD NOT MADE	94
	—	NAMING	95
JULIE WADE	—	LAW OF PARSIMONY	98
DAVID KOEHN	—	THE WINDMILLS OF ALTAMONT PASS	101
MEGAN KAMINSKI	—	[CREASE IN THE FIELD OF MORNING]	102
KRISTIN HATCH	—	BROKEN TULIP	103

—— ART

ARTWORK BY RUSSELL PEAGLER:

AND THAT IS LIFE—RELATIONS	FRONT COVER
AND THAT IS LIFE—RELATIONS PART II	BACK COVER
AND THAT IS LIFE	96
AND THAT IS LIFE—THE COUPLE	97

ARTWORK BY LINDA PLAISTED:

VANISH	36
SHUTTER	37
UPSTANDING	38
PASTURE	39

Greg Grummer Award

Phoebe would like to thank everyone who entered this year's contest. From hundreds of entries, *Phoebe*'s Greg Grummer Poetry Award judge, Carl Phillips, honored the following:

winner:

Angus Bennett—On Whether the River Will Break

finalists:

Joshua Kryah for "My Easter"; "Come Hither"
Eliza Rotterman for "Two Girls"
Kimberly Lojek for "[Draft of Interior System of Structure]"; "[Harnessed Dove and Window Broken]"
Reba Elliott for "Child Not Made"; "Los Mineros para Los Minerales"
Arpine Knoyalian Grenier for "The Cables Set, The Light"
Melody S. Gee for "Migration"
John Pursley III for "[You Can Look Through These Windows—Look, & Not See Anything…]"

I was immediately taken by the way in which this poem pulses forward on a psychological trajectory that's at once clear and yet does not compromise mystery. The poem, for me, enacts the gesture of "I don't want to miss anything," as it shuttles between different markers of possibility—"whether," "if," the periodic interrogative, the sly, unstable punctuation and capitalization (and lack of it), the constant need to look again at what has been seen. The ending feels both like closure and its opposite—resonance, I'll call it.

Carl Phillips is the author of eight poetry collections, the most recent of which is *Riding Westward*. His honors include an Award in Literature from the American Academy of Arts and Letters, a Guggenheim Fellowship, the Witter Bynner Foundation Fellowship form the Library of Congress, two Pushcart Prizes and the Academy of American Poets Prize.

On Whether the River Will Break

on whether the river will break

through aperture into decanted light—

is it the story or the soundlessness

it interrupts you believe in? the cut

therefore the knife? the sky stopped

with cloud is an outline—is

Afternoon, a rinsing of transparencies,

a something lighting on another body,

another lit body and whether the river

will break remains. it rearms landscape,

riverbank with weight—you on

the bridge, poem ticking, ticking.

maybe green fingered grey, maybe lacking

the good hue, unwrung. maybe a quick

air erasing softer edges, a cheek.

waters and you upon them imperfectly.

waters and you (resolving unclearly)

knock against the pilings. what

vanishes behind you is well-dressed,

Afternoon in a strapless dawn-drenched gown.

recollect about you those things (this poem *this*

poem) inseparable from their sounds, bunch them

in a fist until a single heartbeat escapes. eat

it. what is more fragile than Afternoon?

what have I missed? you were there

thinking about whether the river would

break even before I lay claim—

the fish into which your reflection

dissolved? no. surfaced, turned over? no.

re-surfaced. there is water and then a river. river

from a widening of points into a line.

line through another, and then shored-

up bank. distance established further

up one sees or out one looks. that river. any

bridge a sketch of black against the tumble.

I don't want to miss any thing. I don't

want to miss anything. light blocks

my sightline in, overburdening sense.

what if not this? what if not you now?

my cover. the recovery of afternoon.

some wings in motion, then the bird.

some water in motion, then the break.

Two Girls

Our love was an iron bell
unnerved by the train's brazen calls
meat and bones meat and bones.

We spoke like scissor blades
confetti clicking the fan.

I would have stolen two horses
for us to ride up to the ridge

where we might sing
while we pick their hooves clean.

We were tin moths
moving over brick towards the light
meat and bones meat and bones.

Whipping-Bee

All through the whipping-bee, everyone dreamed up
their own bees: dining-bees with heavy silver,
a bee to admire a prodigal child, a caulking job,
a money-bee to counterfeit a mint
or to work the fields at night. People
whip-stitched round the edges of
a quilt of black and gold, raised the frame,
pressed apples from their skins, friends
at least, in willingness to raise and press
and skin, despite their illness of the fastest stitch,
a whisper and spit-house built for karma.
But the whipping-bee was different: people
weren't just labor, rather were the sum
of stings their tongues could make. That's all;
and whether you liked it from silk or needle, leather
or gilt, you knew how much you'd split.
You could not be surprised by the whipping-bee's
results: measured by your pleasure it meant
feeling sore and crabbed next day at home;
the kids announcing they were hitched;
no one able to find the sharpest blade
in the kitchen, chisel gone from the box.

Winter Fiction Contest

Phoebe would like to thank everyone who entered this year's contest. From hundreds of entries, Phoebe's Winter Fiction Contest judge, Nell Freudenberger, honored the following:

winner:

John Blair—The Road to Little Happiness

Finalists:
David Norman for "The Great Basin"
M. D. Baumgartner for "Like Gods of the Sun"
Matthew Goldberg for "With a Mighty Hand and Outstretched Arm"
Pierre Hauser for "Girlyman"
Amy Ralston Seife for "What We Do"
Alison Hicks for "Texture"
Kristie Smeltzer for "Bridges"
Richard Jespers for "Engineer"

The two characters in "The Road to Little Happiness" are memorable not because of their situation—they've just run out of money in Lafayette, Louisiana—but because they have the heft and unpredictability of real people. The readers continue to get to know them throughout the story, and the things we learn are both surprising and consistent with what we already understand. Eddie and Liz speak naturally, often without thinking, and their dialogue isn't burdened by the plot. Things have happened to them, and continue to happen, but they never seem to be racing to execute a predetermined course of action. These characters are low on money and luck; the author doesn't romanticize their plight, but also doesn't ignore the potential for beauty and elation in the midst of their difficulties. While I was reading "The Road to Little Happiness," I had moments of anticipation—what will happen to these people; will things be all right for them?—that are to my mind the mark of the best fiction.

Nell Freudenberger was awarded the 2005 Whiting Writer's Award, the PEN/Faulkner Award for excellence in short fiction, the O. Henry Award for short fiction, and the Sue Kaufman Prize for first fiction from the American Academy of Arts and Letters.

The Road to Little Happiness

Eddie Meers was awakened by the pulsing, plaintive sound of a tractor-trailer rig's back up signal. He put a hand on the steering wheel and pulled himself up to see a truck on the far side of the grocery store's parking lot, backing up to a loading dock on the side of the building. It was early-morning dim outside, everything grayish. He had parked the car on the edge of the lot closest to the road, and now he could just make out SUPER-1-MART on the store's green and yellow façade. Liz lay curled up in the back, still asleep, her breathing heavy and slow.

A horn blew on the road nearby, and she stirred, stretched, groaned, opened her eyes. "Hey," he said to her.

She blinked at him for a moment, still sleep-heavy and dull. A thin woman with gray teeth, looking a little hard-used. "Hey, back," she finally said, her voice tobacco-hoarse. "Where the hell are we?"

He looked around again at the misty parking lot. "The town of Lafayette, Louisiana. Parking lot of a grocery store."

"Yeah, OK then," she said, as if she were used to waking up in the back seats of cars parked in strange Southern towns. She probably was, Eddie thought. He had only known her three weeks, now, and it was likely she'd made many trips like this before she had run across him. They were both old enough to have seen and done a hell of a lot of things, and both weary enough not to care to talk about any of it, much. That was part of what had brought them together. Nothing so attractive as surrender.

She sat up, leaned over the back of the seat. "Hey, how about we go get something to eat?"

"You buying?"

She grinned and he could see the space where a tooth was missing back inside her left cheek. "Hell, no. I don't have one thin dime, as you damn well know."

He smiled, though he didn't feel it. "Well, that puts us just this side of broke-dick, then. I think I got about two-fifty in loose change, and that's about it." He wasn't quite sure where the money had gone. They had left Apache, Oklahoma three days before with better than four hundred dollars in traveling funds, headed for Orlando. They had probably pissed away two hundred in Lake Charles, screwing around in the casinos and getting drunk, but the other two hundred just seemed to have evaporated. Gas, he supposed, and food, and just the usual attrition that went along with getting through a day on the road. Now they were stuck. No money, no gas, no damn pot to piss in.

"I know a place," she said.

"You been to Lafayette before?"

"Nope," she said, and left it at that.

He shrugged, too road-worn and tired to care much. "Well, then, you just tell me where to go."

It was early enough that there wasn't a great deal of traffic on the streets. He drove slowly through town, Liz telling him to turn here and there, looking for something, though Eddie wasn't sure exactly what the something was. He didn't ask; he figured she knew what she was doing.

Liz had him pull up to a curb in front of a Methodist church, a huge building with four tall columns and broad steps leading up to the doubled doors of the entrance. It looked, Eddie thought, like the kind of church that white-linen planters would build, a cross between Tara and a Greek temple. Two black men sat on the steps, smoking cigarettes, watching them pull up. Eddie felt a dart of unease; they looked rough, both of them in jeans and dirty white t-shirts, both of them young but weathered-looking. Eddie had never been comfortable around black men. Indians were another thing. His entire life, he had lived among Comanche, Caddo, Shawnee, Cherokee. Even known a few Delaware and Potawatami. Gone to school with them, got drunk with them. Southern Oklahoma was a mixing-pot Babel of Native Americana. He was a sixteenth Cherokee, himself, on his mother's side. Black men, though, made him nervous. He was twelve or thirteen before he'd ever seen one, and his sense of the world had been set by then.

"Stay here," Liz said, and pulled her door open. Eddie watched her walk up to the men. Neither one of them stood up or said anything that Eddie could hear. Liz squatted down on the steps in front of them. She talked to them, though Eddie couldn't hear what she was saying, made general gestures in Eddie's direction. One of the men said something and pointed down the street, and the other one nodded, agreeing.

Then Liz stood and walked back to the car, both men watching her go. She climbed back in, and he started the car and pulled away from the curb.

"There's a place called the St. Joseph's Diner where we can eat for free, but they don't serve until noon, so we could get some lunch there, but nothing right now."

"A soup kitchen?"

"Yeah, a soup kitchen. You too proud? It's better than dumpster diving."

"Naw, hell, I don't care," Eddie said, though he found he did care, a little. It wasn't something he had thought about before. Bums ate at soup kitchens, but he guessed that was exactly what they were at the moment. Transients. Homeless people. He had never had much, but he'd never been begging before and sure as hell never done it out in some strange town in the back-ass of Dixie. Truth was, he had never left Oklahoma before this, except a couple of trips when he was a teenager down to Texas to go raise some hell where the drinking age was lower. He was forty-six years old, and Liz had come along at just about the time he had decided that that was long enough to live stuck like a powder beetle in a fence post, chewing through every mealy-dull day until it was done, and there was nothing left but to wake up and move on to the next one.

"They said there's another place we might be able to get some breakfast, though. There's a bakery that gives away day-old donuts and stuff, but we need to get there pretty quick, because they only do it at seven and if we're not there then, we're shit out of luck."

"You just walked up to those guys, black guys, strangers on the street, and asked them where to go for a free meal?"

"Yes. So what? You know of a better way to do it?"

"No, I guess not. What if you had pissed them off? What if they'd gotten offended?"

"Then they would have gotten pissed off and offended. So what?"

"OK," Eddie said, because there was nothing else to say.

The bakery was a small shop near the highway, not far from the grocery store where they had parked the night before. The building looked like it had once been a house, and then the highway had brought businesses in around it and it had bowed to the inevitable and itself become a place of business. He turned onto the side street that ran beside it and parked a block or so down.

A half-dozen people were already standing around behind the bakery, in the small area that would have been the back yard when the building was a house, but was now a paved lot with a blue dumpster crouched on one side. Two big pecan trees shaded the area and covered it with leaf litter. Three of the waiting people sat side by side on a low concrete bumper-block, and the other three stood apart from one another around the lot. One old man was crouched down, picking up pecans from the asphalt. There were two women there, one a thin, very tan woman who sat beside a younger black man on the bumper-block. The woman looked the way Eddie imagined Liz would look in ten years of the kind of hard living she seemed to prefer—worn, her face wrinkled to leather from too much time spent outdoors in the sun, the skin around her eyes loose and bagged.

The other woman was much younger, dark skinned but not black, Eddie thought. Mexican, maybe; it was hard to be sure. She stood off to one side with a little girl, maybe three years old, on her hip. No one except the old man with the pecans even looked up when Liz came up, Eddie following along.

The old man looked at the two of them, his mouth open, his head cocked back to take them in. His lower lip hung down a little lower than it should and the eyebrow and eyelid on the same side of his face sagged. Eddie figured the old man had probably had a stroke or something at some point in his life. Or maybe had taken a hard blow to the head. The man held out his hand, showed them the pecans he had picked up. "These are mostly rotten," he said, the words a little slurred. "Left from last year. But there's a still few are good. Ya'll can have these ones if you want 'em."

Eddie would have declined, but Liz said, "sure, thanks," and squatted beside him and held out her cupped hands so that he could pour the nuts into them. He held two of the pecans back, showed them to her, and said cryptically, "I don't want to start from nothin'."

"That's good," she said. "That's smart."

She sat down on the pavement and squeezed two of the nuts together in her fist until one of them cracked. She picked the meat out and ate it rapidly, occasionally spitting out a bit of shell. She did it with considerable skill, and Eddie watched her until the bakery's door opened and she stood up and put the rest of the nuts in her pants pocket. Everyone gathered around the door, where a stout man wearing a dusty-looking apron stood holding a cardboard box. He looked around the small crowd and gestured to the woman with the little girl.

"Bring that baby up here," he told her. "She can have something first."

The baker pulled a white bag out of the box and handed it to the little girl. "Them's good donuts. I made 'em myself," he said to her. He gave the woman two more of the bags. "Them's bagels, in the one, and some raisin bread in the other. You make sure that child eats some of that raisin bread. It's real good."

He handed out the rest of the bags. Eddie got a bag with two bagels and what looked like a blueberry muffin inside. Each person mumbled "thanks" as he or she accepted a bag, and the baker said to each of them, "that's real good; you'll like that." When everyone had gotten a bag, he said, "Ya'll enjoy, now," then went back inside and closed the door. Eddie distinctly heard a dead bolt clack home.

Liz started in on a glazed donut and the old man who had given her the pecans waved his hand at her, made a shoo-ing kind of gesture. "Ya'll ought to go on out of here to eat. They don't mind giving you the food, but they get all pissy if you sit out here and eat it."

"OK," Liz said. "We don't want to make anybody unhappy."

"Sure, sure, just letting you know. Hey, ya'll traveling, are you?"

Eddie answered him quickly, afraid the old man might be looking for a ride. "No, not right now. We're going to be here for a while." He glanced at Liz, but her expression didn't seem to suggest anything one way or the other about the lie.

"All right, all right. Well, that's good," the old man said to Eddie. "Hey, if you want some work, I know about something."

"Yeah? What kind of something?" Eddie stopped walking, and Liz stopped with him. There was an odd sort of energy in the moment, Liz waiting for him to talk to the old man, holding half a donut and watching him. The car was waiting nearby. Calm expectations. They felt of a kind, a unit. Not like husband and wife, exactly, but dependant enough to feel the need for consultation. "I could use some work."

The old man held out his hand. "I'm John Foley. They call me Jack."

Eddie took his hand. The man's palm and fingers were so thickly ridged with calluses that shaking his hand felt something like gripping a crab's shell. Eddie felt a sudden respect for the old man. There was a lot of hard, physical labor in that hand. "I'm Eddie. This is Liz." *We're not married*, he almost said, wanting for some reason to make that clear. Like he was afraid some old fart living on the street would get the wrong idea, make some uncomfortable assumption.

Jack waved at Liz, a small gesture just with his fingers. "Glad to meet ya'll. You seemed to be enjoying the hell out of that donut."

"Sweets just own me," Liz agreed. "I don't hardly eat nothing else." She dug in bag for another one.

"Yeah, you can tell that," he said, and then to Eddie, "well, look, I know some work if you want it. They been tearing down a church over south of town. They got it deconsecrated and all, so there ain't no sin to it. They're building a new one out in front of where it is. They don't want to just knock it down with bulldozers because they're trying to salvage the lumber and the pipes and the fixtures and such out of it. So they're taking it apart in pieces with crowbars and sledges. They got a guy comes around about eight o'clock to a Texaco station down there, he comes by in a truck and takes anyone who wants some work out there to help rip the thing down. They pay five dollars a hour, and give you lunch, too. No taxes, so you keep what you make. It's kinda hard work, but there's plenty of it. And they're pretty good to work for, them being church people and all."

Eddie looked to Liz. "What do you think?"

Liz shrugged. "Up to you. We sure could use the money. I can take care of myself."

Jack grinned, and his teeth were tobacco-brown and gapped behind the drooping lip. "It ain't all that far, but we better get walking."

Eddie took one of the bagels out of his bag, handed the bag to Liz. "There's a muffin in there you'll probably like," he told her, and then to Jack he said, "All right, then, let's go tear up a church."

They waited at the Texaco station with a couple of other men, everyone sitting on a curb by the street. None of them had a watch, so nobody really knew what time it was, but it felt to Eddie as if it must be past eight. The traffic had picked up and it looked like rush hour, everyone going to work.

Jack looked up at the sky. He looked critically at the blanket of overcast, the fog starting to burn through in just a few places. "I think he's running a little late," he announced.

"You think there's a problem?" Eddie asked.

Jack shook his head. "Naw, he's always running late. He's a volunteer at the church. He's retired. He's got no reason to be on time."

"Maybe he's like all of us and doesn't have a watch."

"Maybe. I don't know. I never asked him."

"How long have you been working at tearing this church down?" Eddie asked.

"Oh, on and off for probably three weeks or so. I travel a bit, so I missed a few days. There ain't a hell of a lot of it left, now. I figure they'll keep us at it another two or three days, then get in with a front loader and haul the rest of it off and burn it or something."

"Anything I should know about what we're supposed to do?"

"Naw, it's pretty easy. We're pulling apart the framing right now. You just stick a breaker bar into it and yank it apart, put the pieces in a pile. Be damned careful about where you step, though." He pointed at his feet. "I got some good boots from the Goodwill last year, they got steel shanks in the soles. But there was a fellow over there last week wasn't watching out, stepped on a board and got a four inch framing nail through his boot sole and clear through his foot. He wouldn't let us pull it out. Last I saw of him, they was taking him to the emergency room in the back of pickup truck, that board still stuck to his foot."

"Jesus Christ," Eddie said.

"Yeah, I don't think he felt too good about it, either."

A red pickup truck bumped into the gas station's lot, blipped its horn. "That's us," Jack said. Eddie followed him to the truck and the man inside waved at them all and they all climbed into the bed, Jack and Eddie on one side, the other two men on the other side. Neither of them looked at Eddie; they kept their eyes on their hands or their feet. They looked tired, already, Eddie thought, before they had even started. Used up. Both of them in dirty work clothes, both of them smelling so strongly of old sweat that even the open back of the truck seemed a little close. One was older, one was younger, and Eddie wondered if they might be father and son. Two generations defeated by something, down and out and working for day-wages at tearing down a church.

Eddie had known hard work his entire life, but he had pretty much always had a job of some kind or another, a regular paycheck coming in. Never much. Never enough to get ahead. But he'd always known where his next meal was coming from, and where he would be laying his head on any given night. For the last fifteen years, before he had hooked up with Liz, he had driven a forklift for Goodyear Tire and Rubber, at the big plant in Lawton where they made passenger car tires. It was a fair living.

He owned a little trailer house in Apache, though he rented the lot it sat on. The rent was overdue, and he knew the landlord wouldn't wait long before breaking in. If he were gone long enough, they'd sell the trailer to pay what he owed. He had for the last six years supported his mother in an elder home, which had been a damned expensive proposition. Then his mother had died. He had felt cut loose, like there was nothing left to him but the strange sense of being adrift in a world where every single step he took was one he had already taken a thousand times before.

He had never saved much, and never went anywhere. Every godsent day, he had stepped out of his front door and seen the perfect image of his life: the flat Oklahoma plains, running off in every direction without tree or hill or hope of any place to rest the eye. No place better or worse or even much different, anywhere in sight.

Then he had met Liz at the Maddog Lounge in Lawton, and now here he was, six hundred miles from home, sitting in the back of pickup truck. No job, no nothing. He had used most of what money he had to bury his mother, and that had left him the four hundred he and Liz managed to spend inside of three days. Liz, mostly, doing the spending. She was a woman who liked to live high on someone else's coin, that much was clear.

And the truth was, nothing about that made him particularly unhappy. It was still better than what he had had.

The driver pulled out, heading south, back towards the highway. The traffic was heavy and backed up for a ways behind the stoplight at the intersection before the overpass. Eddie sat in the truck bed, breathing the exhaust fumes. Far up ahead, on the concrete median between the lanes, he could see someone standing, holding a sign. While he watched, the person went up to one of the cars waiting at the traffic signal, took something from a hand held out of a window.

Then the light changed and the traffic started ahead through the intersection. Eddie shifted, turned to look at the sign as they passed by. Liz stood there, holding a paper sign that read

     HUNGRY
     BROKE
     PLEASE HELP
     GOD BLESS YOU.

It looked like it had been written in dark red lipstick, onto a brown paper grocery sack. He wondered where she had gotten the sack. Liz didn't see him; she was looking at the drivers as the cars and trucks went by, and he was sitting low in the bed of the truck.

"You can make some money at that," Jack observed, "if the cops don't shut you down first. People are a lot more willing to give money to a woman, if she's moderately good looking, anyway."

"Hell," Eddie said and kept his thoughts to himself.

Just before dark, Eddie walked the five blocks from the Texaco station feeling sore but reasonably satisfied. He had forty dollars in his pocket. Not all that much money, maybe, but hard cash, hard earned. He wondered if Liz had had much luck at the intersection with her sign. It had been strange and a little shocking to see her begging like that, out on a public street for God and everyone else to see. But then, that was what it had come to, he supposed, and it was more or less his fault.

He turned onto the street where the bakery was and didn't see the car. In fact, the street was deserted; there were no cars at all. He stopped and turned slowly around, looking up and down the street in case he might, in some blind lapse of sensibility, have walked right past it. Then, feeling a little panicky, he walked into the lot behind the bakery. The building itself was dark and abandoned-looking. No one was there, and it was very quiet under the big pecan trees.

What he felt—more than the shock, more than the unbearable, sick feeling of dismay—was pure wonder. It was like the whole world had shifted a degree without him ever noticing. It was like some sly magic trick, like how foolish it felt, when they had disappeared, to have believed that the rabbit or the doves or the pretty female assistant were ever really there in the first place. He thought about Liz and felt a wild shiver of anxiety deep inside his gut. He couldn't think why she might steal the car and run off, but he did think she was probably capable of it, if she thought it was in her best interest to do it. He had no illusions about how much she might care about him, or how deep her loyalties might be. He'd gone into this whole thing with his eyes open, and he knew what was what. He just hadn't much cared at the time. Or maybe he had, deep down. Maybe something like this was exactly what he had been looking for when he jumped off that cliff, quit his job and hit the road with this rough and shadowed woman.

The truth was, her running off with everything he had was probably what he had expected all along. Maybe even what he wanted, if he could even know what he wanted any more.

The air still smelled of yeast and bread and he remembered that he hadn't eaten since the sandwiches the church people had passed out to the crew for lunch. He looked around the pavement and found a few pecans and cracked one and picked out the meat with his fingernail. He put the others in his pocket with the forty dollars.

He walked back out onto the street, looked up and down for any sign of Liz coming around a corner, some flash of headlights or the last bit of sun on the old Chevy's rusty chrome. Don't panic, he told himself. Liz would be along soon with the car, and they'd have a laugh about his being worried. It would be all right. He would tell her about the work he'd done, what it felt like to tear into the boned carcass of the old church, about the satisfying way nails squalled when you pulled a board loose with a four-foot breaker bar. About how when a big piece of lumber snapped open because you pushed the bar a little too hard, the wood inside of it would be pale yellow and smell like new pine, like it had just been cut from the tree, though the church was more than seventy years old. Maybe she would tell him about what it was like for her to ask for money from strangers. He would put his arm around her. Tell her how grateful he was.

He put his hand in his pockets, felt the four tens there, how they were limp and damp with his sweat. Forty dollars was enough to get them to Orlando, he figured, but they'd be flat busted when they got there. Maybe they should stay in Lafayette a little longer. He could get in another day working at the church. He had seen a couple of cheap, run-down motels; they could get a room, if it was cheap enough. Clean up, get a good night's sleep.

Twilight had settled under the trees and one of the row of streetlights began to flicker itself to life, droning like a locust. Someone called and he looked up to see Liz come around the corner, her hands full of plastic grocery bags. His heart seemed to unclench in his chest, like a fist opening. He felt himself grinning, like some sort of witless dumbass being handed a candy bar. He stood up and waited for her.

"The car's not stolen, if that's what you're thinking," she announced as she walked up. "It got towed off."

"It got towed? Where?"

"Right out of here. I think the bakery guy called them. I don't know where they took it, exactly. I called the cops from a pay phone, and they gave me an address and a phone number, but we can't get the car back until tomorrow morning at eight AM. And it's going to cost us seventy-five bucks."

"Aw, Christ. What did they tow the car for?"

"For parking too long where we weren't supposed to park, I guess. I asked the woman I talked to at the police, and she said there was a two hour limit in some neighborhoods. I guess this is one of 'em." She put down the plastic grocery bags she was carrying, set them in a pile on the pavement.

"Hey, look, I've got us some food. Bread and some canned stuff. Some fruit." She touched the handles of the bags.

"You went shopping, after they towed the car off?"

"Yeah, sure," she said, her inflection making it a question: *what's your point?* "We got to eat, don't we?"

"Well, goddamn. That's something. I think I would have killed someone, not bought groceries. I think I would've broken that damn baker's ass. I may, yet."

She shrugged, smiled at him, a tired smile, just the slightest curve of her mouth. "What would making a stink have gotten me? Arrested, maybe. This way, at least we don't go hungry. Being angry don't get you nothing to eat."

"Still," he said, "you just impress the hell out of me."

"Thanks," she said. She sat on the curb beside the bags and started digging through them, taking things out. "Sit down, lover," she said, "let's have us a picnic, right here in Mr. Donut's private fucking parking lot."

By the time they had finished eating, all of the streetlights had come on, up and down the street. A car came by and slowed to a crawl as it passed, the driver staring out the window at them. Eddie stared back, and when he stood up from the curb, the driver hit the gas and the car accelerated away down the street.

Liz put out the cigarette she was smoking, started gathering her plastic bags together. "We better find a place to spend the night."

"What are the chances we could get a really cheap room somewhere?" Eddie asked hopefully.

She laughed. "Thin and none. With your forty bucks, and what I made on the street corner, we've got only about twenty dollars more than it'll cost to get the car back. Even if we can find a room that cheap, we'd be dead broke again."

"So what then? A homeless shelter or something?"

"If there is one, how are we going to find it and how are we going to get there?"

Eddie considered it, gave up. "Beats the hell out of me. What, are you thinking we should just sleep in a doorway or something?"

"Drunks and idiots sleep in doorways. If you don't get thrown in jail, somebody hits you over the head and takes everything you own. Or pisses on you because it's funny. There's better places."

"I was thinking maybe we could put off getting the car back, stay here another day. I could go work at tearing down that church again tomorrow. You could do your thing out by the highway."

She stood and picked up the bags. She glared at him, and he realized that he had said something wrong. "That's not even a part of my thing," she told him. "You think I like begging people for money? Fuck that. I hate it like eating broken glass. I mean, somebody threw a goddamned *beer can* at me while I was standing there. But I made twice as much as you did today, and who the shit is going to hire someone like me for a day to do anything, except maybe whore herself? They aren't gonna hire me to tear down a church, that's for goddamned sure."

"That's not what I meant."

"Meant it or not, now you know."

He reached out, took two of the grocery bags out of her hand. "All right, then," he told her, feeling both abashed and unsettled at the same time. All this was a lot to take in for a country boy from backass-nowhere, Oklahoma. "Where to?"

"I saw a place that might be okay, when I was walking around. It's not too far."

She started walking, and he followed. They made their way through neighborhoods of boxy wood-frame houses, some of them lifted a couple of feet off the ground on red brick pillars, all of them rough-built and weathered-looking. A heavy-set black woman sat watching the street from a lawn chair on her porch. She gave them a little wave of her hand as they passed by. Eddie could feel a liquid kind of weariness starting to work its way up from his feet through every working muscle. He wanted to lie down on the grass somewhere quiet, in one of the narrow little lawns they were walking past. But there was an easy mindlessness in just putting one foot in front of the other, following Liz wherever it was she was leading.

Then they were out of the neighborhoods and onto a wider, busier road. On the far side was a park behind a tall chain link fence, its open spaces deep in shadow. There weren't any lights in the park, but Eddie could make out some playground equipment and, at one end, a low, institutional-looking building that might have been a school, all of its windows dark.

They crossed the street, and Liz went to the fence and walked along it, trailing the fingers of one hand across the diamond-shaped spaces of the wire. "Along here somewhere," she said, and then she stopped. Part of the fence curled up on itself, pulled loose from the bottom of one of the steel fence posts to make a low, triangular gap about two feet on a side.

Eddie looked up and down the street, at the cars waiting at the stoplight at the end of the block. "Shouldn't we just find the gate?"

"Parks have curfews. We don't want anybody to see us going in." She tossed the grocery bags she was carrying through the hole in the fence. "So we better do this before somebody drives by and wonders what we're up to."

The park seemed to be deserted. The small lot was empty of cars. Liz went straight to the playground equipment, passing through the hanging chains of the swings and around a domed jungle gym to a wooden play structure behind it. Eddie had seen them before in parks—there was huge one in Lawton—and this was a fairly small example of the type. At its center was decked platform made of two-by-fours, about six feet off of the ground. A plastic slide came off of one side and a climbing net made of chain sloped up to another. The other two sides had low wooden walls and the platform was roofed with a kind of planked steeple, painted red.

Liz set the bags up onto the platform. "We're home."

Eddie had to admit, it was a good place. Well off of the damp ground, high enough to catch a breeze, which would help keep the mosquitoes off. A roof if it rained.

Liz hung the grocery bags from the cross-chains of the climbing net. "It'll help keep any animals from getting to it, and there's too many fire ants around to keep it in here with us," she told him. "Fire ants are the worst if you have to sleep out on the ground somewhere. If it's real dry out, they go after your eyes and mouth for the moisture while you're sleeping."

Eddie squatted down beside her. "You don't think the cops patrol this park?"

"Probably. But they won't bother getting out of their cars to look up here, I don't think."

A whispery curl of paranoia eddied up through Eddie's chest. Abruptly, he felt *tenuous*, as if anything at all could sweep him away, a breath, a gust of wind, the smallest current of the world's compelling disapproval. "You slept in a playground before, haven't you?"

"Once. And on lots of floors. A couple of times under bridges. Lots of times on the ground, out in a field somewhere. When I was a kid, my family used to travel and pick vegetables, tomatoes and strawberries and such. Sometimes, we'd sleep in the fields. That's really not bad if the weather's good. It's kind of nice sleeping out under that stars in a big open field somewhere, especially after it's been diced. The ground smells kind of clean and fresh in a dusty way, kind of like new-mown hay, but different. Good soil is pretty soft when it's just been turned up. Makes a great bed, real comfortable. Sleep like a baby."

"You like sleeping in dirt?"

"Don't knock it 'til you've tried it." She sat down on the edge of the platform, let her feet dangle inside the squares of the chain net. Eddie looked around the dark corners of the park one more time, and then sat down beside her.

They sat without talking for a while, sharing a cigarette and watching headlights flickering through the trees by the fence, the traffic signal cycling at the intersection.

Liz sighed. "It's funny, you get to where it doesn't seem all that bad. All the crap, all the working your ass off and still barely making it. Or you get crazy-assed angry. I've known some people like that, just so poisoned by how much the world pisses on them they can't hardly live. Go around hating everyone and everything because they live in shit and some people live in palaces. Other people, though, they're happy just to have enough to eat and a decent place to sleep. I've been both kind of people at one time or another. Being angry wears you out. It's easier to let it all go."

"I never thought about it much, I guess."

"I bet sleeping in a playground is changing your perspective."

Eddie smiled. "Yeah, maybe. I swear, being with you, I see how dinky-shit I've lived my life."

She shrugged, looked down at the long shadows beneath them. "Some things happen, make you realize bitterness don't do you a bit of good.

Sometimes things happen and you wish—" Her voice trailed off.

"What?" he asked, and she looked at him, a quick, oblique glance, and even in the dark, he was struck by how sorrowful she looked. Black eyes, beautiful and sad in that weathered face.

"I was just thinking of something."

'Tell me."

She shook her head, and he thought she looked like she might start crying. It was a strange sort of expression on Liz's hard face. She bit at her lip, and then said, "I was just thinking about my little girl. Sometimes shit like that just pops into my head, if I ain't careful."

"You got a daughter?" he asked, surprised.

"I did. I don't any more."

She didn't elaborate, and he didn't ask. They sat quietly. After a while, she kissed him, and went back to the corner where the two walls met and lay down. Before long, she was asleep.

Eddie sat alone on the edge of the platform, looking out into the night. He felt chilled, though it had to be ninety degrees out. He climbed carefully down off the platform and walked out across the parking lot and down the road leading out of the park. He stopped just inside the gate, which was open and unlocked. The moon was high now, round and gray as a fish's eye, and he lay down on his back on the road under the sullen Louisiana stars and thought about Liz and her daughter. He wondered if the girl was dead. He had a feeling she was.

He thought then about his own mother, who had moved years ago into dementia until she seemed not to know anyone at all, not even Eddie. Who in the end had wanted, he knew, nothing more or less than to be left alone. What difference had it all made, in the end, love and a child? Not damned much.

Nearby slept another child's mother, curled up alone on a playhouse floor. A woman headed to nowhere in particular, just going to be going. Lost as anyone else. And here lay his own mother's son, who wanted nothing more than to forget about it all, to go on driving south to Orlando, and then past, until he couldn't drive any further. Then maybe he would just walk out into the warm Atlantic and never look back.

The pavement was still hot, still radiating the day's dose of hard summer sunlight. It felt penitential lying there in the grit and the gravel and the heat, flat on his back in the middle of a road. He considered the fact that some bubba in a big pickup truck could very easily come roaring through the gate and run him over without even seeing him lying there. Or that cop making his rounds that Liz had mentioned.

He wondered what it would be like, to be dead. Gone. Disappeared. Darkness and silence forever. He tried to imagine what it felt like to die. Probably not a whole lot different, he thought. Just less worrying about every damned thing.

He took a deep breath and let it slowly out. The moon hovered directly over the tip of his nose, dragging its haunted eye up over the bayous and swamps. To hell with it all, he thought. He hauled himself up off of the pavement and started walking back to the playground. "Eddie?" Liz called as he walked up.

"Yeah, it's me," he called back. She was standing beside the platform. "I was worried," she said. "I didn't know where you went."

He felt enormously tired. "Yeah, sorry. I just kind of went for a walk."

"Are you OK?"

"Getting that way," he told her.

She touched his cheek. "It'll be all right," she said. "Ol' Liz's here for you, cowboy, so don't you worry. Come on and lay down. I'll rub your shoulders."

He did so. She hovered over him, her hands working his sore muscles. It felt outrageously good to have a woman minister to him.

"Can I ask you a question?"

"Sure. Shoot," she said. She sat back, searched around for her cigarettes, tapped one out.

He dug his lighter out of his pocket, held out the flame to her, watched her light up. "What is it you want with me?" he asked.

She shrugged, took a deep drag, let the smoke slowly escape from the side of her mouth. She seemed to be thinking on it. Finally, she said, "See, the problem with people is, they want too much. They always want everything there is. Everywhere you go, all anyone wants is to ride a long greased rail right into the Big Happiness."

"So what do you do?"

"You take a good look, see how things are. Then you grab on to the Little Happiness like a monkey on a mango."

He considered that. "That's what this is?"

"Like the man said, 'Don't want to start from nothing.'"

He put his arm around her shoulders. "That's good," he said. "That's smart."

He knew that he would never go back to Oklahoma. Little Happiness is where I'm headed, he thought, and it sounded like one of those dumbass town names you run across on the road, like Okay, Oklahoma or Lollipop, Texas. Little Happiness, Florida, USA. Glass half full, or some small part full, anyway. Nothing wrong with that.

But there *was* something wrong, when you thought about it. It came to him what the truth consisted in, and it wasn't settling for whatever you had, for whatever damned thing drifted your way. The fact was, a little happiness wasn't enough and never would be. Wanting is all you were, when it came right down to it.

He felt Liz's small hard bones pressed against him. Nowhere you need to be except here, he thought. He closed his eyes and tried make what he could of that small comfort, for as long as it would last.

The 12 or 14 Stations

Melancholy	The grey cloth we crawl upon/featureless terrain Waterloo 8 a.m.
Surprise	The train door that bears our soul away/a gust
Worry	what of ourself remains
Contentment	passing/thin bank at the river bend/wading cattle
Anxiety	Roar of the approaching/news reaching the valley Night caller
Forgiveness	that we cannot of ourselves/or others
Regret	one moment decided/or another
Misery	Not to notice/that the rain we need is at our heels
Sadness	leaves/returning home/ward journey
Happiness	jewel light on water/softly on the way
Anticipation	dressing/fruit trees for the festival
Hope	in Youth our energy
Misery	to turn away from the world
Regret	in age our energy
Hope	her message

Cryptogogic Glossolalia

Prophecy of the denounced Pentateuch
(speculating sensations)
Instant Interregnum, God Falls.
in the space between I and the say-word
I stands for proximity (temporal/spatial)
I manners of clouding—opportunity to
I progress—Memory of—Sleep
I beach approach—cobbled—articulates
I body members parts—focused on
I object(s) of desire—pen knife
I girlfriend, success (as seen)
Collared for the photograph—Which
defining moment—they don't recall
displaced now into the future of the photo-event
Jesus was an acolyte—Or The Paparazzi
Unpopular as guilt—What is German for Bumblebee
German Bumblebee (look it up)—A sculptor (Physician)
Dedicated to the single project of depicting human expression
Physiognomic distortion such as the sneeze withheld—
Or the unpleasant odour. What is the isolated voice
I wonder.

I manage to have written a number of books without
Starting perhaps
Here I start again

What are we to do with these people
Some we love, respect, know something of.

My habits of knowing have crumbled
Lack of attention perhaps. Lack of results.

Those whose desire I have loved—or
I mean those whose love I desire

Of them I grow tired perhaps

Earlier. Perhaps not that much Earlier
I believed I might occupy a number of glamorous Houses.

If we have to choose, what criteria can we trust
As we change—are deflected—deflated—repeated.

The afternoon manages to be the most usual part of the day.

Domestic architecture—cheaply reproduced but functional.
Victorian artisan—a certain skill, a certain pride perhaps.

Those that are tired of their lives—those without a sense of
How to make a decision. They all have no time.

Those that are loved in success. How does it happen—for whom?
Where are my own simple pleasures? What did I give them away for?

Be vigilant—The same room in five years is not the same
room. You are shorter—your eyes dimmer.

For some reason—political acceptance—I have forsaken
The songs of beautiful girls.

Young men overcome their duty with energy.
Here I am again surveying the remnants of the slaughter.

One sees the hideous hermit crabs, four rayfish and
A red gunnet, wings tipped with violet and blue.

If you had time you might devise a method of escape
But you would never be brave enough to attempt it—even
Supposing that it might work.

The Day

If there is a self it hovers so close or so far from us that we cannot know it. That which we tell ourselves about ourselves might be useful about being, might be coincidental with some truth—but we cannot know. For truth also is so close or so far from us.

<u>The Day (A 600 page poem written about one day)</u>

The Dream opening
The acceptance of waking
Leaving the first room
Attending to food
Memories of earlier days
That which needs
The first half-capitulations
Dressing
Tasks
Sleep comes upon him
The tasks
The call
Awake and leaving
Interaction
Escape
The world
Confusion
Love
Intercourse
Retreat
The ambiguous
Loathing and loathed
Selfhood persistent
Fear of death (commitment)
Acknowledgement of Life
Sanctuaries

Work
Forgiveness/generosity
Happiness/tiredness/sadness
The formal retreat
Depletion of energies
The feast
Death

"Vanish"
-Linda Plaisted

"Shutter"
-Linda Plaisted

"Upstanding"
-Linda Plaisted

"Pasture"
-Linda Plaisted

FROM BESIGNED

"If the the text is in cipher, lean on the zeros. . ."
    Edmund Jabes

He writes: Limb washed. Shore, sand, allay, for castles, a pond—who made the garment,
its mouth unmet? Now down the side, whose is it among arch and tier, altar & the white-
  laden word?

He writes: I. Hear the master passing through, footprint left by a step on any leaf,
high air, grass & lungs, fingernail tread & threaded.

He writes: The. Water's lung to lessen the sky, jelly fish, pouch of pouch gone;
small eddies where the cries steeple, white paths left here to find at tide time

Breath awakened, broken by mouth piece; there—cracked pails of avowal,
jellies are light made corporeous where sonic blues like milk, where no ocean keeps.

He writes: With so much. Open, found with so much sand digging, sky will accept us,
bathing the living around its dome, limb under, compact & instrumental

He writes: O. You who study this book rounded at the edge & broken
the faithful body shapes itself along those unmentionable protrusions.

Decide to keep me, show me a many-pronged leech & powerless.
Writes: don't please imagine, bite-mark planted at the crown, clams bleating their pearls

In the cleaving to tractate, trumpet is bell, transparent where foam is conceived.
He writes: Whose find. Of that droplet coursing, whose finger from the pond rings at tide

Harvest Sun

black feathers. cropduster. white rain.
        the callus of father's hand. eyes like warm resin.

the salt of wet lips. mother's breath on her cheek
        cooling the burnt surface of touch.

the scars on mother's palm like letters of holy books.

        ~

she will wake to the thrush of beating wings. crow caw.
        clank of plates. her mother's humming.

will smell the oil-piquance of frying chorizo.
        burnt tortillas on a stove.

with her finger
        know the white

of lilies. trace the transparencies
        of linen.

a glass of water breaks. spills
        light sewn into light.

she will feel for the shards with her hand
        as if touching for a newborn's lips.

        ~

sweet garlic, blue corn, butter,
        the past frets in her mouth like a tongue.

she rubs her eyes, the surface
        of the cornea burns, petaless.

fingerprints of moisture
	on the glass she has touched.

she touches her lips,
	peels chapped skin from the skin.

	~

her hands will read the shape
	of thyme and prayer,

of plum stone, flesh, stone,
	of salt, tomato, burning,

of cornhusk, pesticide, blossom,
	of mother, azalea, ash.

her right hand will hold to prayer;
	her left will let go.

The Aerialist Pays a Visit

I am a catch, the trap. The bar, a cage. Is a cat. Is a
key. Release. Magnetic feet pull, O different world.

World of mine, so sleepy—how odd. All the soft
questions. Pulling up window, I tumble out.

Outside, our show snores midnight rumble. Brides
rest tight in beds, no question. Father echoes: *married*.

Marry Andrei, how. To be less tangible, slip of a girl.
Cracked hands trail the cage. Lion rumbles gentle.

Gently, cage pulls hand, pulls key. To slip inside,
to spread his jaws, crawl head into mouth on fire.

Fiery cheeks, a baptism, a name: *Talia, crushed*. My
Jack blamed, my burden. Shame. Tumble the lock.

Lock to key. A trap, my feet. This world no different
from the rest. Blame me: the cage, the cat, the release.

THE SECOND COMING OF AFRO-CHRIST

The second thing everybody noticed when Jesus came down from the spaceship was the size of His afro. I mean, it was HUGE. Jumbo-halo-sized. Like Dr. J back in the day. Which got me to thinking about all those old paintings, and then it hit me: So *that's* what all those halos were about. *That's* what they were trying to say. It was huge, but it was tight, too, just like in the paintings. And all that hair looked *killer* with that white robe. I declare, He was one fine-looking black man!

The spaceship, white like a floating spoonful of sour cream, just showed up out of nowhere. Nobody knew it was coming, or at least if they did, they didn't let on. One minute there was no spaceship, and then the next minute—BAM!—there was this spaceship hovering eight inches off the ground in Iceland and popping out this Black Jesus like it was some kind of holy toaster. But the most amazing thing was that they got it all live on cable. From Iceland! When nobody knew He was coming! Now how do you think they managed to pull *that* off?

I was in the barbershop when it happened. When we got a look at burnt-toast Jesus, everybody got real quiet for about two seconds. Then everybody *exploded*. We were all high-fiving and yelling, "I *knew* it! I *knew* it! What they gon' say *now*, yo?"

Everybody crowded around the TV, and we watched Jesus float down from the top of the ship, but His robe was so long that you couldn't tell if He floated all the way to the ground or if He just hovered there. You could tell that He was tall, though, maybe six-foot-eight, even allowing for the size of His afro and the possibility that He might have been floating just a little bit. He looked like a power forward, like Antoine Carr in 1987, except with a lot more hair. Then He held His hand up, and you could see for sure that He would have no problem palming a basketball. Everybody got real quiet, like God had told them to shut up, which I guess He had. Then He said two words. His voice sounded like a trombone. "VICTOR PARNELL," He said. Then He floated back up over the top of the ship, hung there for a second like Jordan in his prime, and then *zip*. He was gone.

Now *everybody* in the barbershop was *totally* freaking, because Victor Parnell? That's me.

***

Dead silence. Everybody just stared at me. I tried joking that Jesus had to be talking *Iceland*-talk, and *that* was why He happened to say something that *sounded* like Victor Parnell, because, I mean, of all the names in the world, why would He say *mine*? Didn't make any sense. The fellas agreed with me because most of them had known me all my life and they knew I hadn't ever done much of anything. So we went back to watching the spaceship, which was just sitting there in Iceland. But fifteen minutes later, six black Suburbans screeched up to the barber shop, and all these white men in suits busted in with guns, and they didn't even have to say anything before everybody pointed at me. Ten minutes after that, I was flying in a helicopter, strapped down with a bag over my head. I don't like to fly, and I had never been in a helicopter before, so I was sort of glad about the bag over my head, but I was pretty scared, I don't have to tell you. These white people had guns! As far as I was concerned, they might as well have been the police! And who knew where they were taking me? I didn't know what was going on, but I was pretty sure about one thing: You can't fly a helicopter all the way to Iceland!

When they pulled the bag off my head, we were at the city airport. I looked around at the white men in suits. "You didn't want me to see how to get to the airport? You think I don't know where the airport is? You think I don't know that you're taking me to Iceland?"

"We want you to know what we want you to know," one of them said.

They put me on a plane, and they gave me a nice suit of clothes to wear, just like what all of them were wearing, but they gave me all these little cameras and microphones and scientific instruments to wear, too, and I'm thinking, they're trying to fool Jesus! I sure hope He doesn't think any of this was my idea! But then I remembered that God knows *everything*, and I wasn't too worried. And then I realized that God even knew what I was going to say to Him when I got there, so I tried to stop worrying about that, too. But the white men hadn't got this all figured out—I reckon not too many of them went to church much, even though they had the clothes for it—so they thought talking to me before we got there might actually do some good. It was like I was in *Mission: Impossible* or something.

"Victor Parnell?" one of them said. He had on a different suit from the others. His voice sounded familiar. I think he was the vice president. It was funny to see him in real life because he looked like somebody you might see at the hardware store looking for parts to fix a toilet for the first time.

"Yes, sir?"

"You know anything about this flying saucer business?"

"Only what I seen on TV."

"You had any contact with aliens before?"

"No, sir. But He didn't look like an alien. He looked like Jesus."

"At the present time, we cannot confirm. It could be Jesus or it could be somebody tricky—which is not to say that Jesus couldn't be tricky if He wanted to, assuming, of course, that trickiness is not inconsistent with His other godly attributes."

"But God can be whatever God wants to be, right? He done pulled some tricks in the Old Testament. How 'bout that burning bush?

He cleared his throat like he wasn't sure what to say next.

"Aliens are tricky, Russians are tricky, Chinese are tricky, Arabs are tricky. See what I mean? There is *no* shortage of trickiness in this world."

"Yes, sir."

"Look, Victor, I'm going to be straight with you. All the seals in Iceland are dead."

"Say what?"

"A few minutes ago, this alien, or whatever he is, he killed all the seals in Iceland. He proclaimed them dead, and then they were dead. It was just Iceland, you understand, and it was just the seals, because he says he's just *a little bit* angry right now and this is just *a little part* of his wrath, because he says he wants to see you *now* and he doesn't know what the wait is all about."

I looked around me. "This the fastest plane you got?"

"We had to have time to talk to you first. Get you wired up and all that."

"You think that's a good idea? You trying to outsmart Jesus?"

"He might not be Jesus. He might be an alien."

"You think aliens can kill seals with words? You ask *me*, that sounds like God talking."

"Look, we've got scientists, historians, theologians working on that angle. If they say he's Jesus, then—"

"He's Afro-Jesus," I said. I didn't know what was coming over me.

It was like Afro-Jesus was making me say these things. "Call Him Afro-Jesus."

He stared at me for a few seconds. Looked like he wanted to bite a rock.

"*Fine*. He's *Afro*-Jesus, and here's what we need you to tell *Afro*-Jesus about America and about our plans for a renewed and renewable alliance with the Almighty."

I listened to what the man had to say, even though I knew I wouldn't need any of it, that I wouldn't use any of it. If Afro-Jesus had wanted to talk about that stuff, then He would have asked for the president. But He didn't. He asked for me. Me, Victor Parnell. I knew that Afro-Jesus had other things He wanted to talk about. I just had no idea what they could be.

***

When we got to Iceland, they took me in an ambulance from the airport to the spaceship. There were bunches of people there praying and singing. I would have sung, too, but I couldn't remember the words to any hymns. I mean, I *know* me some hymns by heart, but my mind was just this *hum*.

Stairs came down from the ship and I thought He was going to pop out and get me, but this voice in the hum said, "Come." I think I was the only one who could hear it because as far as I could tell, I was the only one who could hear the hum, and the voice definitely came from the hum. I took a deep breath and looked around at all the folks looking at me. They'd all gotten quiet.

"So long," I said.

I was real nervous, but I tried to look hardcore when I went up the steps, like I had a six-pack of death strapped to my hip. I didn't want to look like no punk on TV because if I did the fellas back at the barbershop would never let me live it down.

When I got inside I expected to see all the usual spaceship stuff you see in movies, blinking lights and things, maybe with some of them big-head aliens running around, but there was none of that. It was just like a brother's crib. Posters of dogs playing poker. Some African art. I wanted to turn and run, but I heard the voice again—"Come!"—so I kept walking until I came to this great big round room in the middle of the ship. In the center of the room was this Huey Newton chair with Jesus sitting there in His white robe and platform heels. And His hair was *perfect*. Or at least I thought so at the time.

"J-J-Jesus?" I said. I sounded like one of those scared white people who die in horror movies. I tried to keep my knees from knocking together, but then I remembered that you can't fool Jesus.

"Victor Parnell," He said, and His voice was like warm butter flowing all over me and I tasted popcorn in my mouth and started crying.

"That's my name," I said. "That's my name."

"I'm hongry," Jesus said. "You hongry?" That's the way He said it, too. *Hongry*.

"A little, I guess." I remembered that I hadn't had any lunch *or* dinner.

"Let's have some sandwiches."

I expected Him to, like, just *speak* some sandwiches for us, sort of the way He just *spoke* all those seals dead, but He took me down into the kitchen.

"You're wondering about the crew," He said. "You're wondering if I got Me any big-head aliens." He was bending over in the refrigerator.

"Yeah," I said. "I mean, *yes*. *Yes*, Jesus."

"No crew. You think God needs a crew? God don't even need a ship, but people can process only so much out of the ordinary. You know why?"

"Cognitive dissonance," I said, even though I had no idea what it meant. I don't even know where I got the words from. They were just in my head, in there with the hum.

"You know it," He said.

Jesus pulled out a whole bunch of sandwich meats and cheeses and lettuce and tomatoes and onions and these big hoagie rolls. We made us some dagwoods.

"I love a good sandwich," He said. "And I know you do, too!"

"I guess you know everything," I said.

He shrugged. "Pretty much. And you folks only know what I want you to know. All them wires and things they put on you under that suit? I got 'em broadcasting *I Love Lucy* instead. Right now Lucy's working the assembly line! Ain't that one a *stitch*?"

Jesus laughed and the hum got louder. I laughed, too, one of those belly laughs. I thought, *I'm laughing with Jesus!* Then I laughed some more.

My sandwich was pretty good, but I was so nervous, I thought I might not be able to keep it down.

"Relax, Brother Parnell," He said. "You're gonna be just fine. Now tell Me, what's on your mind?"

"Don't you already know?" I said.

"If I want to, sure. But I can choose not to. I got Me a switch I can turn off. Imagine Me trying to have a conversation, sitting there trying to listen when I already know every last word I'm gonna hear. I couldn't stand it! So, right now, I can't tell a thing about what you're thinking. I want *you* to tell Me what you're thinking."

"Well," I said, but I couldn't think of another word to say. I just kept thinking, *I'm eating dagwoods with Jesus! I'm eating dagwoods with Jesus!* Then it came to me. "I know!" I said.

"Yeah?" He looked excited.

"Why am I here?"

"You mean, *why-am-I-on-the-planet* here or *why-am-I-on-the-mothership-with-Jesus* here?"

"I'm starting to think they might be the same thing," I said. And then I looked around the kitchen. "This is the mothership?"

"Today it is," He said. "You know how it works. The ship is in My *mind*, so it is whatever I think it is."

"Does that mean I'm in your mind, too?"

"Something like that."

This was getting heavy. "Am I *always* in your mind, or am I just in your mind right now because I'm inside the mothership?"

Jesus waved away the question. "Best not go there, Brother Parnell. You know, cognitive dissonance and all that."

I nodded. The hum got louder.

Jesus pushed away His plate and belched. It sounded like Wynton Marsalis blowing a long, sweet note. "Let Me ask you a question, Brother Parnell. How many people on earth are descended from Adam and Eve?"

I thought about it for a second. I'd always wondered about that Adam and Eve story, about whether it could be true just like it said in the Bible. But if Jesus was asking me about it, I thought it would be best to give the Bible the benefit of the doubt.

"All of 'em?" I said.

"That's right. All of 'em. The power of geometric progression."

"Okay," I said, not understanding but then understanding through the hum.

"Now check out this list: Adam, Samson, King Ramses II, Helen of Troy, Confucius, William the Conqueror, Rapunzel, William Shakespeare, Thomas Jefferson, Frederick Douglass, and Wilt Chamberlain. Now tell Me: How many people do you think are descended in a direct line from every last one of those people?"

I didn't know what to say. I wasn't even sure who some of those people were.

Jesus went on: "The Almighty Supreme Sovereign of the Universe orchestrated the fates of nations, the lives of millions, to create one perfect man, a man of integrity, courage, decency, and common sense—*one man* who is descended *in a direct line* from every last one of those people! And that man, Brother Parnell, is *you!*"

"*What?*" It took a second to sink in. "You mean to tell me that *Wilt Chamberlain* was my *daddy?*"

"Brother Parnell! Let's look at the big picture here! You have a special purpose! You are the culmination of a plan that God put into action way back when Adam and Eve got kicked out of Eden!"

"What? What plan? What purpose?"

Jesus sighed. "I don't know."

"You don't know? How can *You* not know?"

"Because the switch is off, remember? And because what was supposed to have happened didn't happen. We set everything up. The perfect man, the perfect day. Two things we didn't take into account, though."

"What's that?"

"Free will," He said. "And drugs."

It sounded like an accusation. "I don't do drugs," I said.

Jesus smiled. "Maybe not today. But what about on April 9, 1983?"

I could remember a few things about 1983. I was in my sixth year of junior college, working on my A.A. in criminal justice. I could picture the faces of two or three young ladies from about that time period. Some barbeque floated through my mind, but that might have been from 1984. And that was it.

"I suppose I might have smoked a little weed back then," I said. "But

I have no idea about April 9, 1983."

"Oh, Victor," Jesus said. "Victor, Victor, Victor. How *could* you? *That was your day!*"

"It was?"

"Oh, yes, it was. Matter of fact, it was THE day."

"It *was?*"

Jesus laughed, but it was a sad laugh.

"Come on," He said, getting up from the table. "Let Me show you."

I grabbed the rest of my dagwood and followed Him.

***

"I could just show you this in your head, put it in there with the hum, but that's been known to make people go crazy. Sit down."

We were in a little theatre with only two seats and a big screen. It felt wrong to sit down before He did, but He insisted.

"Now, this may freak you out just a little bit at first, but you'll get used to it."

"Okay," I said. Dag, I thought. If *Jesus* thought I was going to freak out, then I was probably gonna freak out *good*. I grabbed the armrests of the chair.

He sat down, the lights went out, and the screen lit up.

It was a movie of me in 1983, and I was glad He didn't show it to me in my mind, because it was hard enough to handle on the screen.

I watched me get out of bed. It was like there had been a whole camera crew in my apartment that day. I watched myself do everything, even sit on the toilet. I got kind of embarrassed at that.

"Can we skip to the important part?" I said.

Jesus laughed. "Just wait," He said. "It's coming."

I watched myself sit down and drink a glass of orange juice. My hair was looking pretty ratty. I had a big afro back then, even though afros had gone out of style. None of that jheri curl nonsense for me! Watching the movie, I remembered that I spent a lot of time back in 1983 working with my hair, picking it out in front of my mirror, patting it down. Sometimes, if the weather wasn't just right, I wouldn't even go outside. It was weird looking at myself from so long ago, when my face was so smooth and my hair was still mostly on my head. Now I had an Uncle Remus hairdo, just that fringe. I sat there in the dark and rubbed the smooth top of my head.

I watched myself go down to the diner to get some breakfast. There was a fine waitress there named Shirelle. I kept trying to talk to her, but she wouldn't give me the time of day. I realized now that it must have been my hair. I had the Locomotive Breakfast—*Big Enough to Pull Your Train ALLLLLL Day Long!*, it said on the menu. Then I went down to the park and watched the fellas play some ball. Usually I would play a game or two, but that morning the line for next game was about fifteen brothers long, so I went over to the chess games and watched some of that. I never quite understood chess, but I liked to listen to the oldheads talk smack to each other while they hit that little clock. Then me and Tyrone, one of my boys from the junior college, sat on a bench and watched the ladies.

I said to Jesus, "Didn't I ever study?"

"Never on Saturdays," He said. "Hang on. We're almost there."

Then I went to lunch at the Burrito Palace. All the girls who worked there were Puerto Rican. I tried talking to them, but they all pretended like they didn't know English, which was bull because I had seen some of them around the neighborhood for years. Then I went to the record shop and looked through the jazz albums. I talked with Billy behind the counter for a while. Billy used to be in the record business. He played saxophone, did some session work. He could show you all the albums he played on. When his boss left for lunch, we snuck into the storeroom and shared a reefer.

"Drugs," Jesus said, shaking His head.

I felt so bad right then I wanted to hang my head in shame for sure, but the movie was still going on. It was kind of boring, but it was incredible, too. I was up there bigger than life.

Then I went to the Cut Shop. Finally, I was gonna do something about my hair. The place was packed. Saturday afternoon and all the guys were getting their trims for the club that night. All the oldheads were talking politics and sports as usual. They were working Ronald Reagan up one side and down the other. Ronald Reagan was the best thing to happen to barbershop talk since Muhammad Ali. I picked up an *Ebony* and flipped through it.

After a while, it was my turn. Most of the guys could cut heads pretty good, but Old Man Reese was the one you wanted. A lot of the fellas would wait an hour just to get Reese. But I didn't get Reese that day because I waited. I got Reese that day, I realized, because God wanted me to.

"Victor Parnell, you sure *need* Reese today!" he shouted when I got up out of my chair. Everyone laughed. "Matter of fact, you might need Reese today *and* tomorrow, rough as you look! Boy, you been sleeping in a bush?"

I laughed along with everybody else because Reese was the master, and if he gave you a hard time it was because he liked you—and because he knew that only *he* knew how to fix your hair. Sometimes one of the other barbers would look at a brother, shake his head, and point to Reese.

With Jesus, I watched the master go to work.

"*Look* at him go," Jesus said, leaning forward in His chair. "Reese was good, but that day he had the Spirit!"

The shop started filling up. People were coming in off the street just to see what Reese was doing. People started going, "Mm-mm-*mm*!" and "*Work* it, Reese!" Somebody even shouted, "*Testify*, brother!"

But I just sat there in the barber's chair with my eyes closed because I was still buzzing off that reefer I'd smoked at the record store. At the time, I didn't see Reese dancing around me with his trimmer and his brush and his scissors. When he finally stopped, the whole shop got quiet. Then he leaned forward with his scissors and snipped one last hair.

I liked to have a heart attack waking up to the noise of the shop. People were clapping their hands and shaking their heads and hooting and hollering.

I watched myself in my confusion. Damn, my hair looked good, though. I mean, it looked *perfect*. I looked over at Jesus in the dark and I could see the halo of His afro. It looked almost as good as mine had that day. *Almost*.

"Keep watching," He said without turning to look at me.

I watched the rest of my day. All the fellas crowding around me after I got out of the chair, spinning me around, holding mirrors up to my hair, reaching out to touch it but getting their hands slapped away by the other guys. Reese refusing my money when I tried to pay him, instead taking a bunch of pictures, promising to put me up on the Wall of Fame, where he kept pictures of his best cuts. "In fact," he said, "I'm gonna take everybody down but YOU!"

When I left the shop, three of the brothers went with me. They were calling out to people on the street to check out my cut.

"Victor Parnell is coming!" they were shouting. "Victor Parnell with the perfect afro! Ain't never *been* an afro like this before! Ain't never gonna *be* an afro like this again!"

And then the movie stopped and the lights came on and Jesus was looking at me.

"And they were right, too," He said.

I rubbed my eyes against the light.

"Do you remember what happened the rest of that day?"

It was just now dawning on me what kind of trouble I might be in.

"I—I don't know," I said. And it was true. I remembered the cut, but not the rest of the day.

"Well, to make a long story short, you felt kind of sick when you left the Cut Shop, so you decided to go to a movie, and then you went to a club and hung out at the bar for an hour, and then you went home. Alone. And then you went to sleep."

"That's it?" I said.

"That's it. You had the perfect afro—an afro that it took thousands of years to create!—and you spent the rest of the day in the dark."

"Oh," I said. "You would think that one of the ladies at the club would've noticed."

Jesus shook His head. "And do you remember what happened the next day?"

"I remember!" I said. And I did. "I woke up and—and my hair was all tore up!" Now the movie was playing in my mind. "It was like I'd never had it cut in my life! And—and there was hair all over my pillow!" I gasped and looked at Jesus. "No!"

"Yes!" He said. "That was the day you started losing your hair."

"But why? Why *that* day? Why give me perfect hair for only one day?"

"When much is given, much is expected. You, Brother Parnell, were a one-man city upon a hill! You were the finest specimen of human manhood the planet had ever seen! All that blood flowing through you, the blood of William Shakespeare, the blood of Wilt the Stilt, but with a haircut that left Samson and Rapunzel in the shade!" He held out His hands. "And what did you give to the world that day? You gave the world nothing. You and your drug-addled brain spent the rest of the day in the dark. *In the dark*, Brother Parnell."

That's when I started weeping.

I don't know how long I cried. It could have been a century. It could have been longer. But when I stopped, I felt His hands on my head.

Jesus said, "Don't cry, Brother Parnell. Yes, it is true, I *am* a God of vengeance. But I have already taken your hair. *That* was my vengeance upon you. But I am here now because I am also a loving God. A forgiving God. A God of second chances."

His hands were warm on my head. I felt that butter feeling again, tasted the popcorn. Then the hum in my head went away. And the sadness in my head went away, too.

Jesus said, "Rise, Brother Parnell! Rise and go forth!"

I rose up, not knowing what I was supposed to do, just knowing that I had to trust Him. Jesus led me to the door of the mothership. We were standing just outside the view of the singing, praying crowd. I could hear that there were thousands of them now. I wondered how long I had been in the ship.

I looked down at my clothes. I gasped. I was wearing a white robe, just like His.

I turned to Jesus. "What do I say?"

Jesus smiled. "You will know," He said. And then He was gone.

I was standing at the top of the stairs now. The sun was dead high in the sky and everyone was wearing sunglasses, all the media and the men in suits and the praying, singing thousands of people. But when they saw Me, people shielded their eyes like they were seeing a nuclear explosion. All of that light—from the sun, from the ice, from the ship, from the white of my robe—all of that light was focused right at the top of my head. Then I heard people yelling and pointing and shouting that they wanted to touch it.

I didn't have to look at my reflection to know what they were talking about. I could feel that perfect golden halo all around my head.

I held up my hand and everyone got real quiet.

"My name is Victor Parnell," I said. "Do not be afraid."

Translated by Kathleen McGookey

GRANDMOTHER

L'aïeule

Tous les jours, ils s'en vont. Elle reste seule à la maison, inutile.
Aujourd'hui, dans le coin du gamin, elle a vu un brouillon, elle l'a lu, elle a même corrigé cinq fautes. Heureuse, elle s'assoit, ses pommettes sont roses. C'est si rare qu'elle fasse quelque chose.
Elle ne sait comment le dire au garçon quand il rentre, il entend cette joie qui ne peut sortir, il l'aide: mais voyons! c'est tout le contraire, elle lui a fait gagner une heure, il a tant de travail!

Grandmother

Every day, they leave. She stays at the house alone, useless.
Today, in the boy's nook, she saw a rough draft, she read it, she even corrected five mistakes. Happy, she sits down, her cheekbones pink. It's so rare for her to do anything.
She doesn't know how to tell the boy when he comes home, he hears this joy which cannot emerge, he helps her: but no! It's quite the opposite, she helped him save an hour, and he has so much work!

GEORGES GODEAU

Translated by Kathleen McGookey

Perplexity

Perplexité

Baptiste le maçon est vieux, il voyage en groupe. Comme les autres, il achète une carte pour son neveu avec des montagnes, des lacs. Lui dire qu'il l'aime n'a pas d'allure. Et signer tonton, ou Baptiste… L'homme fait une croix en branlant la tête.

Perplexity

Baptiste the bricklayer is old, he travels with a group. Like the others, he buys a postcard with mountains and lakes for his nephew. Telling him he loves all this lacks style. And whether to sign Uncle or Baptiste… The man makes the sign of the cross while shaking his head.

"THE KANGAROO OF ETHEREAL POSSIBILITY"

Review of: *You Don't Love Me Yet*
&
Interview with Jonathan Lethem

"I think it's time Wendell Maas had a little visit from The Shadow."—Pynchon, *The Crying of Lot 49*

Often compared in part to Don DeLillo and Thomas Pynchon, Jonathan Lethem has been visiting his quirky superhero, science fiction, world-of-possibilities on his faithful readers since his debut novel *Gun, with Occasional Music*, published in 1994. This novel, frequently cited as a "Chandleresque" science fiction detective story features a hard-boiled detective, (who has literally lost his nerve-endings to a girl from his past), and who must now get to the bottom of a sordid cover-up in a world where animals have become genetically altered members of society and people take government-sanctioned drugs increasingly composed of a substance called Forgettol.

From his debut novel on to *Amnesia Moon*, a short story collection called *Wall of the Sky, Wall of the Eye*, and *Girl in Landscape*, Lethem refined his aesthetic of story telling and dealt with themes of memory, memory loss and obsession. In particular, a short story called "The Happy Man" deals with the idea of repressed memory, our individual hells and the human ability to adapt and cope with separation as the protagonist finds himself raised from the dead by the government, but forced to spend a portion of his time in Hell. While in Hell his body is functional but catatonic and his son traces the time he spends in Hell via computer simulation.

Lethem captures an ability to write about obsession most poignantly and hilariously in his third novel, *As She Climbs Across the Table*. In this romantic comedy, Lethem creates a university environment similar to DeLillo's College-on-the-Hill, where particle physicists have created an absence in space and named it Lack. Unfortunately, for Philip Engstrand, a professor researching conflict between the disciplines, his girlfriend and physicist Alice Coombs falls absolutely, obsessively and exclusively in love with Lack. Unfortunately for both Philip and Alice. No matter how often Alice offers herself to the anomaly, Lack refuses to accept her, and Lack never changes "his" preferences in terms of an object originally scorned.

***

Jonathan Lethem was born in 1964 in Boreum Hills in Brooklyn. He is the author of nine books and was named in 2005 a recipient of the MacArthur Fellowship, often called the "genius award." In 1999 Lethem won the National Book Critics Circle Award for his novel, *Motherless Brooklyn*. This work, featuring a protagonist detective named Lionel, who struggles with Tourette's Syndrome, not only won Lethem acclaim but also began Lethem's most noted series of works dealing with biographical themes and material.

In a scene where Lionel leaves Kimmery's apartment to pursue the mystery of Frank Minna's death, he describing himself as the Green Hornet, a hardened man in a collared, black coat, ready to fight crime. However, Lionel soon revises that description, acknowledging the tics he fights against to maintain clarity and focus that make him feel like a "whole nest" of hornets, rather than a crime-fighting hero.

This mixing of Brooklyn, superhero comics, and pieces of biographical material became signature aspects of Lethem's next works: *The Fortress of Solitude, Men and Cartoons* (short story collection), and *The Disappointment Artist* (collection of essays). A true fan of the Marvel Universe, Lethem uses superhero lore for both texture and the advancement of themes. Two notable characters are: Black Bolt and Omega the Unknown. Black Bolt, the silent leader of the Inhumans, is forced to remain mute due to a voice so powerful that a single uttered word could shatter the world. He serves as the favorite character to Rachel Ebdus and Mingus Rude in *The Fortress of Solitude* and the Dystopianist's rival in *Men and Cartoons*. Another obscure superhero, Omega the Unknown is less characterized for his striking superpowers than as an embarrassingly boring comic with an unbelievably limited run. (Both also made Lethem's list of "Top 5 Most Depressed Superheroes.") In today's current age of Marvel Comics, thriving on the popularity of Spiderman and the Fantastic Four, Black

Bolt and Omega appear to be forlorn role-models uncomfortable in their powers and largely forgotten or unknowable. Lethem uses these qualities to communicate themes of powerlessness and identity confusion in *The Fortress of Solitude* and longing in *Men and Cartoons*.

However, it's not all comic books for Mingus and Dylan. In a Powell interview, Lethem refers to *The Fortress of Solitude* as an "oceanic book." The narrative is wildly imaginative and eclectic, spanning 30 fictional years but also dealing with biographical information from his childhood growing up in Boreum Hills in Brooklyn during pre-gentrification, confronting issues of race, artistic auteur and musical history. Mingus and Dylan must deal with their separate formations of a racial identity, an artistic identity in the graffiti world of tagging, and their choices of friends, music and drug use, not to mention the magical properties of a ring which literally allows the characters to fly or become invisible as "Aeroman."

The themes and material of *The Fortress of Solitude* also bleed into the short stories in *Men and Cartoons* and the essays of *The Disappointment Artist*. In the funniest story ever written featuring a giant paperclip and a superhero named Super Goat Man, Lethem further explores the idea of comic books as childhood mapping and contemporary mythology. In a story entitled "The Vision," the main character marvels at re-acquainting himself with a boy from school who used to dress up in the red face paint and android melancholy of the superhero, The Vision.

However, in his most recent novel, *You Don't Love Me Yet*, released March 2007, Jonathan Lethem takes a self-proclaimed movement away from comic books, superheroes and Brooklyn to the sunny, sexy and bizarre world of performance art, zoo-keeping and a band with intellectual property rights concerns in LA.

***

The novel opens on an epigraph of two different songs with the identical title "You Don't Love Me Yet." In the opening chapter Lucinda and Matthew are introduced as they sneak through the small door of a cube in an art exhibit to have sex for purportedly "the last time." Although Lucinda worries about

Matthew, it is not due to the break-up, but rather his concern for a female kangaroo named Shelf who has ennui.

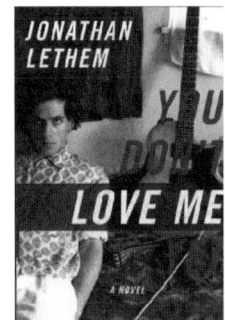

Matthew's story takes an odd turn down the road of marsupial kidnapping, while Lucinda becomes increasingly involved and obsessed with a man she refers to as the Complainer, particularly after she appropriates the words of his complaints into song lyrics for her band.

The band composed of Lucinda, Matthew, Denise, and their shy genuis, Bedwin, is hired to play at a performance art party where everyone will literally be dancing to their own music, received through individual headphones. It is to be a party where the band plays silently as a visual backdrop, and the food and drink is never offered to the guests. Once this party mysteriously transforms into the band's big break, the foursome must deal face to face with the Complainer, his "monster eyes" and ominous insistence to his intellectual property rights and a nebulous share in the band's destiny.

Some questions this novel poses are incredibly funny and self-aware, while others are funny and heartbreaking. Can Lucinda regain control after her affair with the Complainer? Does the kangaroo, Shelf, suffer from ennui because of a sense of entitlement and unattainable expectations? Does a band need a name? Can you "be deep without a surface?"

In this new novel, not only does Lethem depart from superhero themes, but he also develops a sexy, irreverent and killingly funny voice, replacing nostalgic longing with racy confusion and existential doubt. In just such a moment of doubt, Denise comes to the rescue: " *'We can all move into my apartment,'* said Denise. *'We'll be one of those bands that's also a utopian collective, an experimental group marriage, and then we can all kill one another' "(97).*

Lethem, Jonathan. *You Don't Love Me Yet.* New York: Doubleday, 2007.

AN INTERVIEW WITH

Jonathan Lethem

-photo by Sylvia Plachy

In your new novel, You Don't Love Me Yet, *you take a self-proclaimed departure from familiar material such as: Brooklyn, Blues and Black Bolt (the Marvel Superhero condemned to silence lest his voice shatter the world). Did this transition to different material feel painful or organic?*

Both organic and necessary, I'd say—but there were still moments of awkwardness or distress in making the transition. Of course, I was as much making a return (to California, to romantic comedy) as I was a departure (I particularly associate this new book with an older one called *As She Climbed Across The Table*) but after ten years of working in the vein of the Brooklyn books (which is to say not just Brooklyn, but childhood memories, fathers-and-sons, '70's pop culture references) (and which consists of not just the two novels but the story collection and the essay collection, which both make use of the same materials) I was a little disconcerted to let go of it, for sure. Not only can it be quite pleasing to be acclaimed as the "Faulkner of Boerum Hill," but the autobiographical and testimonial intensity of the previous novel carried with it a certain addictive feeling of significance and duty. I felt that *The Fortress of Solitude* was a kind of collective oral history of the neighborhood. *You Don't Love Me Yet*, by contrast, was defined as a project by a sense of freedom from responsibility to any external truths—I was ready to reassert my privileges as a pure storyteller, and dwell in that wing of the house of fiction where story, character, and incident are their own reason for being. As I worked, rediscovering this freedom felt better and better.

Also unlike Motherless Brooklyn, The Fortress of Solitude, Men and Cartoons *(short stories), and* The Disappointment Artist *(essays), the new novel,* You Don't Love Me Yet, *has a different tone. Although the characters and cover art are definitely angsty, there is a certain feeling of lightness and relief in kangaroos, sex, alcohol, performance art, and the riddle/slogan: "you can't be deep without a surface." What is most important to you in/about this novel?*

Well, I think it is my funniest book, and my sexiest. Lucinda came to life for me, as a character, as fully as any I've written. And I'm particularly proud, yes, of the book's surfaces—the sentences, the paragraphs, the metaphors and similes. And despite the apparent avoidance of "deep" or "personal" material, the book, for me, very effortlessly encompasses a fund of very affectionate nostalgic material—it encodes a lot of what I remember most fondly about myself and my friends in the Bay Area in the late eighties and early nineties.

Much of your work, from As She Climbed Across the Table, *to an essay on viewing* Star Wars *twenty-one times, to the new novel, deals with the idea of obsession. In* As She Climbed Across the Table *Alice Coombs is a particle physicist who falls in love in an unswerving, unrequited, and obsessive fashion with a void in the universe the scientists call Lack. In* You Don't Love Me Yet, *how does Lucinda's obsession for the Complainer, which in many ways is no less self-destructive, differ from Alice's obsession?*

Nice spotting—I think it's extremely similar! The Complainer is precisely a kind of human void, who tends to give back reflections and echoes, albeit more distorted ones than the enigmatic silences of Lack. What I like so much about the comparison between the two books that you're suggesting here is that I remember well how difficult I found it to portray Alice Coombs' experience in any direct way—I felt I was more or less bluffing through those few sections where she defends her obsession directly to the narrator, Philip. My ability to inhabit Lucinda's obsession more fully describes my progress as a writer in a most particular way.

Similar to Vonnegut, your novels are rife with shared details that form a sort of web connecting the body of your work. For instance, Black Bolt is the favorite character of the Dystopianist's rival in Men and Cartoons *and Rachel Ebdus' favorite comic book character in* The Fortress of Solitude. *Also, the last line in the lyrics to the song "The House Guest" in* You Don't Love Me Yet *is a favorite phrase of Frank Minna, ("I'll sleep when I'm dead"). Even more strange, the female kangaroo with ennui in* You Don't Love Me Yet *appropriates her unusual name, Shelf, from the "Hitler Cat" Kimmery is house sitting for in* Motherless Brooklyn. *Are these details part of the conscious or subconscious construction of a personal mythology, the structuring of a universe between your work, or merely the invention of an overactive "mining" of the material?*

I have to admit that there's less heavy intention behind these echoes than you might imagine, though I do take pleasure in the fact that they reward a close reader of my work with a series of 'recognitions'—in a way, the most important effect of the echoes (some of them made consciously, many others unconsciously) is as a kind of 'how do you do' to the close reader, a way of acknowledging that they and I are in a conversation that extends beyond the frame of any single book. Plus, I think it's funny.

In You Don't Love Me Yet, *the band, (who can't settle on a name,) has a hit song called "Monster Eyes." The genius of the song is that everyone who hears the lyrics taps into the theme of the destructive nature of love, but everyone has the same reaction: "It's about all of us! But it's about me most of all. . . . It's most particularly about dangerous me." It might not be the most original question, but with "You Don't Love Me Yet" as the title, and failed love as another recurrent theme in your work, what do you think about the possibility of love in the modern world with the above, seemingly universal, perception of self?*

Well, I suppose that the book's conclusion (and thinking-in-fiction is the only form of philosophical speculation I do, on the subject of love or any other) is that love, like art, is an attempt at human connection—and, therefore, tenuous, enchanted, and, yes, worthwhile; but also a process, a constant coming-into-being, rather than an endpoint or a destination. Spooky enough for you?

With Joey as the kangaroo in your debut novel, Gun, with Occasional Music, *and Shelf as the kangaroo in your latest,* You Don't Love Me Yet, *which is your favorite kangaroo?*

My favorite kangaroo is neither my first kangaroo nor my second, but rather my next kangaroo, the beautiful kangaroo on the distant horizon, the kangaroo of ethereal possibility, the kangaroo towards which I have been moving all my life.

And Our Brains Have Sailed Away

And our brains have sailed away,
What used to make us tick.
Is it luck or a roundelay
In an endless Stooges flick?

What used to make us tick
Was the mark of a cultured mind.
Not the endless Stooges flick
Where your forebrain's your behind.

In the dark of a cluttered mind,
Curly and Larry and Moe,
Where your forebrain's your behind
In the culture's afterglow.

Curly, Larry, Moe,
Nature's pentimenti!
In the culture's afterglow
The current cognoscenti.

Nature's pentimenti!
Who says we're out of luck,
The current cognoscenti?
Nyuk nyuk nyuk nyuk nyuk.

Who says we're out of luck?
Is it luck or a roundelay?
Nyuk, nyuk, nyuk, nyuk, nyuk—
And our brains have sailed away.

The Boy President

When you saw that small boy
down by the railroad tracks bent low,
his whole body focused for once
on some important task, you probably knew
he was lining Lincolnhead pennies
to smash on the iron rails.

In the trees beyond these rails
there's a lidded bucket where the boy keeps maps
to countries he made up in his head. He stores
rusty safety pins, piles of zippers,
and broken light bulbs, filaments filling
a Styrofoam cup. All the glow gone out of them.

But look closer:
it's not coins but crickets he's lashing
to the tracks, their bodies immobile
and bound in blue fishing line,
eyes like tiny moons orbiting a lost planet,
thin copper bodies shining in the dark.

To Katharine: At Three

As if you could ride into the piazza
with the four horses of San Marco, ride
with the organ and five bells, as if
you could ride past the clock that sings
with the tide, sings with the sun, sings
with the ships and the moon, as if you could ride
your painted horse into the lagoon,
its red boats and striped oars, as if you could
light lanterns, straddle boards, there are flowers
at your feet, and you ride under the Rialto,
the Scalzi, under the Bridge of Sighs, your horse
plunging into the shuttered night, the canal
now rising, you gripping the reins under a carousel sky,
your breath a flame, my rippled star.

To Walt Whitman in Winter

Stoked
the pig iron wreck
of what you are

sledge of sleet
the miles the rails the Union
Pacific

Glacier with a cow-
catcher

how many harps
run over

& wit, the conductor?

This must be the engine
that frosts

this the igneous
that rides on lava

this the scream of a revelator
gone deaf in white

On the Excision of Man

Into the mangrove the propeller stalled

& the petered-out momentum
carved
as if it followed a hyphenated line

magic-marked on a manatee
spiral blade gutting
until the contents (under pressure)
escaped like a can of Alphabet

Soup & the skin shredded, felt like
a man-of-war

You could repeat this Act / trap door into histrionics

inasmuch to say the water evermore emerald
(the whirl ubiquitous)

THE AMBIVALENT

*

Adore: Reject

*

The sustenance, reality, is amoral
        Beauty and horror:
        Not shame, power:
            Both and neither:

*

Irresistible season, the wind, the leaves
a longer sleep, a furtive once-only
                inevitable allure

Autumn. Ripened to the core. Plucked.
Belonging, the very fruit.
Old poet: I am mostly sad. Mostly.
The sun is bright. But my heart, the wind
in my veins.   Core: bless me.

*

Jung on Schopenhauer: *Here at last was a philosopher who had the courage to see that all was not for the best in the fundaments of the universe:*

Earthworms tormented to death by ants

*

Horror: kiss me, I love you: beauty
Beauty: desire the loss of all clothes: horror
Core: the heart beating faster all day, I wish I never touched you.

*   *

Beautiful or disgusting
How *complexio oppositorum*
is any given moment: *all things*
possible in the fullest meaning of the phrase

*

As a dying person has little muscle
and cannot control
and there are holes throughout the internal body
the decay happening where it wants
the gums, the organs, the skin between the toes

He said, the problem is when one person
doesn't know when the theater is over.
Wanting: nothing is hard.

*

Horror: The foreground of wonder
Beauty: *Think not of them, thou hast thy music too*
Both: Just how much pain.

Your Boarders

It is too personal

you are right

the repeats the betrayals

soon vanish soon enough

The taste of candied orange like holiday

varnish honeycombed

misstatements and mistastes

and the sound of

the break from the

body but shhh

you are safe

A swarm of a swan of

pinpricks

and thimbles you know hat boxes and

other horrors

like re-death

like abnormally ill-written destiny

a continuous thaw without end

but soon vanish very hard

to understand without brain

nervous system or body but shhh

you are safe

When the world turns back

the grey curtain

back door fence line trees

who can see

in colorless glistening needles

the colorless sunrise that

will not vanish

out of the stained night

misimagined

in red that worthy that desire that nothing

there, yes, you are safe

The Good China

Peter's defense was passive. He held up his arms, stepped from side to side, and stood back from the offensive player, as though pantomiming an invisible wall, relying on the gesture to block the shot.

He played basketball like it was baseball, John thought— hugging the space around the net like it was second base; running away from the other player, rather than getting in his face; always worried about being tagged by the ball.

John bunny-hopped backward, and let the ball go in a perfect arc into the net.

"Eleven-four, you," Peter said, clearly more interested in ending the game.

"No, no," John said, scooping the ball from the ground and checking it back at his son, whose slight frame and made-for-basketball height resembled his own. "That was a walk. You have to call those, Pete." He flicked the basketball pole with his fingernail and the hollow, metallic sound lingered rudely. Whenever he came off of a lay-up, or a rebound, and found himself under the net, John always flicked the pole—counting coup on his opponent, turning an ordinary game of drivewayball into an all-out melee.

Peter dribbled the ball with his right hand, holding his left out loosely while his dad shuffled around him, stabbing the air with his hands, which, if nothing else, achieved the effect of distraction. Though already well behind the three-point line, Peter moved backward farther, out of his dad's range, practically standing on the sidewalk, and took a shot. It fell short by a full yard, and John easily seized on the rebound. *Ding!*

But instead of ending their eleven-point game with a bank shot from the three-point line, as he was positioned to do, John moved in next to Peter, his elbow extended out, to block him. "C'mon, Dad. Let's finish this," Peter said.

"Why so eager to lose?" John said. He dribbled low to the ground, hunched over.

After teasing Peter with the ball for a while, John shouldered him out of the way for a lay-up, and the ball rolled off his fingers into the net. "Good game," said John.

"Yup," said Peter, starting to head inside, where his mother, Abigail, waved at them from the kitchen window. Peter waved back.

"Hold on," said John. "Stand next to me. I'm gonna teach you how to shoot."

"That's okay, I'm good," Peter said, lingering at the door.

"You're *not* good. That's why we gotta do this," John said to the back of Peter's head. Peter stood next to his dad, holding the ball. "This isn't baseball. Don't keep your eye on the ball. Keep one eye on the net, and one on the other guy. When you shoot, don't aim at the rim, aim just above the rim. And don't go for those lazy bank shots—"

"I got two of them past you," Peter reminded him.

"Don't brag; you're embarrassing yourself," John growled.

Peter tossed the ball with both hands, and it swirled around the rim before spilling over to the opposite side, where John caught it. "Don't shoot yet!" John said. "Listen to what I'm telling you. After the ball leaves your hands, you're not done with the shot. The most important thing is the follow-through. It doesn't matter where you're standing, or what kind of shot you are making. The most important thing is to follow through; otherwise, you have no control whatsoever. And the name of the game is control."

"Really? I thought it was basketball," Peter dead-panned.

"Smart-ass."

Recently, Abigail started volunteer work at the Center for the Disabled. The year before, she had tried building HUD houses, but found that, without experience or, at the very least, body bulk, she was a mannequin on the construction site, modelling work clothes. She had been present for the ground-breaking, but hadn't even been back to that neighborhood since the building began. They offered her a secretarial role in the HUD office, but she couldn't imagine spending her time away from home in that way. If she was going to sit at a desk, she was going to get paid.

Abigail found her work at the Center for the Disabled more fulfilling on a personal level. At the CFD, she was physically useful to many people, several times a day. When Richard, a man in a wheelchair, passing her in the hallway, dropped his book on the tile floor, Abigail leaned over to pick it up for him.

"Thanks," he said.

"*Hamlet?*" Abby asked.

"Can you believe I'm reading it for the first time?" he said. He was the director of the CFD theatre troupe. "I've been around for sixty years and never read *Hamlet*."

The troupe was practicing to perform *Rosencrantz and Guildenstern are Dead*. The director's name was Richard, like the Shakespearean king, a fact which the troupe exploited on days when he was behaving particularly monarchical. He was one of the less disabled members—they are called "members," Abigail noted, as if the CFD were an exclusive country club—so he helped organize events and activities, and acted somewhat like a staff member himself.

A group of seven less-disabled members had been putting on productions in the summers for a number of years, and somewhere along the line had committed exclusively to Shakespeare, and Shakespeare-related plays. Originally, the performances were just weekend entertainment for the less-abled members, but then, when members began to invite their families, and family members began to invite friends, it became a community staple—an anticipated public event. They started to sell tickets, so that when Abigail got involved, during the Fifth CFD Summer Shakespeare Festival, it was also a cash cow.

"The ending isn't a happy one, I'm afraid," Abigail said. "*Everyone* dies."

"I like that," Richard said, and smiled like he'd just heard a bit of good news. "Just like real life."

With his wife away from home three evenings a week, John lapsed into a regressive bachelorhood. He still shouldered his share of the housework, which consisted of lifting himself up long enough to put the trash out by the curb, but other household things were left unfinished; even, occasionally, the cooking. Sometimes it was too much of an effort to make food. Sometimes it was too small a reward to eat it.

Taking out the trash, John began to realize, was what he contributed to the family labor. Even Peter—who, ever since school ended, had made a suspiciously successful effort to avoid going out to eat at the diner with his high school friends—managed to leave the dishes in the dishwasher after dinner, where they waited for Abigail to turn the machine on at night. But taking out the trash—that was John's business.

Sometimes he woke up early and watched as the trash truck emptied his two mismatched aluminum bins, the way Abby used to watch Peter and Gina, eight years apart, mount the steps of a bus every morning. He tried to construct in his mind what Abby was doing now. The best he could muster was a blurry image of Abby sweeping the stage, dusting the props, and making sandwiches for the actors.

When Abigail first began volunteering, it had sounded to John like a decent thing to do with her time. Then, when it began to intrude on their personal life, John started thinking of the idea of working without pay as slightly offensive. When he thought about it now, it was almost an insult, for a man who had worked his whole life to maintain an upper-middle class salary, to have his wife go off and work for nothing. As though she were subtly communicating to him that the way he spent his days was worthless, a hobby, just another way to pass the time.

At first, Abigail was flattered that the troupe was trying so hard to draft her onto the stage. But then, though she hated herself for thinking it, she was also horrified by how easily they assumed she would fit in. It was a paralyzing thought, that this was the company to which she belonged—a company of the slightly less disabled.

Abigail was never involved in drama—had never been in a play, even in grade school. Once, in her last year of college, she fell abysmally in love with an actor named Connor, going so far as to move in with him, against the advice of her parents. He had a tortured childhood—a topic to which he could steer any conversation—including one story that he often repeated about a crazy religious mother who burned things, which Abby assumed to be apocryphal. He had a drug habit that made him even more aloof, and therefore more enticing to her, at that age. In those days, Abigail saw her quiet tolerance of her circumstances as heroic, and it was not until Connor invited his ex-girlfriend to live with them in their apartment that her heroism was tested, and found wanting.

After leaving Connor's apartment—that very day in fact—Abby met John at the public library, and was so startled by his uprightness, his maturity, that she promised herself in that moment she would marry him if he ever asked. She needed to be *good* to herself, she decided. She needed to find a *good* man, for a change, and then to hold on to him. So she was stunned when he asked her to marry him, that very week, over brunch at the Rue de L'Espoire. It was a fancy-casual French restaurant (they served duck, but they also kept ketchup on the tables).

She didn't understand quite why, but it was this same feeling that struck her now, as she debated whether to join the troupe of the slightly less disabled. That she *ought* to do so. That it would be *good for her*.

Driving home with the sun still high in the sky unsettled him. It was seven in the evening, and John felt a vague desire to drive around a while before returning home. Night, at least, would have presented the day with a choice of finality. But driving home from the office with the sun still piercing through the windshield, after working a solid block of ten hours with no natural light, he could no longer pretend to be lost. The path home was too clear.

First, he reviewed the events of the day in his head, and chastised himself for all the little things he'd left undone. Then, finding Peter napping on the living room sofa, he felt his son's idleness as a rebuke to him. John stood looming over him, his suit jacket folded over his arm, for longer than he needed in order to ascertain that Peter was sleeping. Several things occurred to John at that moment: that standards of living are on the decline; that he *wished* he could sleep all afternoon; that he would not be able to use the sofa to watch television or read the paper (which he'd left unfinished from that morning, anticipating the moment when he would arrive home from work to an empty couch).

John had the habit of yelling, and apologizing immediately, before Abigail even realized that she had been yelled at. It was a marital habit—complicated, evolved, and bearing no resemblance to behavior that he would have exercised in other circumstances.

As Abigail slipped out of her clothes and into bed, she asked John why, in all their years of marriage, he hardly ever talked about his family. He shrugged. Then, after a durable silence, she asked whether he had called the phone company about a questionable charge on their bill. He acted as though provoked. "Look, I may be old, but I'm not senile. Gimme a break. You're not so young either," then slid seamlessly into the apology. "I'm sorry, baby. Come 'ere." And Abigail would let herself be held, feeling whiplashed by the change in mood.

Her friend Jen, the armchair psychologist, had unofficially diagnosed John as bipolar. But Jen used bipolar to describe anything with contrasts. The decor in their house was said to be bipolar. Her manual shift Volvo. The modern world. The Old Testament God.

"She has *got* to find a new adjective," Abby remembered thinking at the time, but wondered too whether, in just this one instance, it might not be appropriate.

The basement door—the door that led to Peter's underground bedroom—opened, and he heard footsteps walking down the stairs. With no guests at all that summer, he wasn't accustomed to hearing footsteps on the stairs. His dad leaned over the railing. His hair was flecked gray, and his chin was glistening with aftershave. He wore a suit jacket and tie. It was always a surprise to see his father in the morning, fully awake. As though he embodied a different possibility of who he might have been.

"Make a plan," his dad said.

"Huh?" His eyebrows raised, Peter looked up from his book.

"Don't be thick, Pete. You heard me." John began to walk back up the stairs.

"Dad?" Peter was so disoriented, between reading Vasari's *Lives of the Artists* one moment, and being brow-beaten by his father's anger the next, that he literally felt dizzy. John paused on the steps. "Uh… can we talk about it?"

"What's there to talk about? You're not going to live in the basement all your life. So you might as well start now. Just make a plan, and follow through with it. It doesn't matter *what* you do, as long as you stick with it long enough to carry it out. You know what I'm saying?"

Peter stared at his dad as though he didn't, in fact, know what he was saying. He hadn't dressed or brushed yet, so he lay there skinny in his boxers and tee, and he had a fuzzy look to him that looked stoned. "Do you want me to find a job?" Peter said.

"Hey, there's a plan!" John walked down the stairs and leaned on the railing.

"But where would I work?"

"Peter. I'm only gonna say it twice. It doesn't matter *what* you do, so long as you do it, and follow through with it."

John and Abby sat on opposite sides of the bed, half-turned toward each other— an awkward pose that looked like two nudes modelling. It was three AM on the digital clock, and they had been talking, without facing each other, since ten.

"*I'll* move out," John said.

"No, you wouldn't *adjust* well," Abigail said. "Let me find an apartment. I've seen a few places along Blackstone Boulevard I wouldn't mind renting."

John sniffed. "I forgot about Blackstone Boulevard." Only the year before, they had purchased a burial plot along that same wide street, which bordered the river.

"It's not like we have to sell everything. Actually, I'm kind of looking forward to living on a tighter budget. It'll be like college."

John cast her a hurt look, which she either ignored, or didn't notice.

That night, they had said the things that they'd spent years trying not to say. Abby was trailer trash. John was a robot. Abby was just like her mom, acting proud when she had nothing to be proud about. John had tedious habits and no energy leftover from work for his family. Her ambitions to save the world were laughable. His moods were worse than a premenstrual teenager.

When John first began dating Abigail, he should have known it wouldn't last. The last twenty-six years, he figured now, were borrowed years. She had a touched quality, a hovering-above-life smile. In an odd way, it had always been the agreement—they raised children together, until the children were no longer children. At which point the contract on their marriage would be reviewed. The way she carried herself said she had never "settled"—not really. It was only luck that he had met her coming off of a bad relationship with an actor. Now, he figured, she was simply cashing in on what fate had promised. He was almost excited for her—for what she might do next in her life—except that he hated the thought of Abby alone. Or worse, of Abby not alone.

John began throwing things away as though he had a vendetta against common household objects. Anything that he couldn't remember using in the last year, he disposed of, regardless of value. He decided that they only needed two of each dish in the house, so he purged the house of its excess dishware, including the good china—a wedding gift from Abby's brother.

He had thrown away so much, he thought, it should be easy to keep track of what was left. He set to cataloguing the objects in his house, marking what belonged to whom, and where it could be of most use. When it came to clothes, John suddenly couldn't tell what belonged to his son, and what to him.

He found a desk set that he bought for Peter when he was fourteen, but never used. John himself had been impressed by how compact it was. How little space it occupied. He took it out of the shrink wrap, and fastened a nib to the tip of the pen.

He decided to compose a letter to his wife, which he could only recall doing once or twice before throughout their marriage. It felt awkward, writing "Dear Abby…" as if John were one among thousands of letter-writers, clamoring for her advice.

John wrote that he wished he could take back the things he said, and that he wished he could learn to communicate. He wrote that he knew now why she always asked about his dead relatives. At the time, he mistook it for a morbid curiosity, but now he thought she may have wanted some assurance, that if she were to suddenly drop off, someone would still remember, and talk about, *her*. So he wrote to her about his family.

He wrote about his grandfather, who came to Providence from Corsica on a rickety boat, and became the first Italian millionaire in New England, recycling paperboard before anybody knew what recycling was. About his dad who became the first of his family to go to college, brokered for a while, invested his money in stocks, bonds, start-up companies (some good, some bad), and left John with just enough to raise a family on. About how John himself never had a head for business, and decided as a last resort that civil engineering is something he could live with. "Once in a while," he wrote, "I get to see a dam or bridge that I helped engineer, and it's almost like I built it myself."

He ended with, "In a month, our son is going off to school and studying art. To be an artist. At art school. I don't think he or Gina will ever have children of their own. But, then again, at least he's doing *something*. I just wish that *something* didn't mean the end of the Gray family line, our prosperity. New money, old money, no money. That's what's become of our generations."

But he tore it up before sending it. He laughed at how pathetic it was to write a letter in the modern world.

Abigail drove through Silver Lakes. Her big brother Ron—the kind of old-school, unapologetic racist you never see these days—used to call this neighborhood "The Swamp" because, he said, of all the "mud people" who lived there. Blacks, browns, and yellows. This was going to be *her* neighborhood soon. She stayed on Blackstone Boulevard just long enough to make John comfortable. Now, she wanted to be close to *the culture*. "Culture," Ron reminded her over the phone, "is what they call it when they grow mold in a dish."

On the way to her new apartment, she passed the HUD house she had almost helped build. It was flat-topped and squat. It had one bush and one window. All she could think about was how happy she was not to have taken part in the building of such an ugly house. Sure, somebody would call it home. But it looked to her like a social security building. Something functional, designed by engineers. Utterly indifferent to beauty.

Instead of going to RISD, John's son went to a no-name art college in San Francisco. Here they were in Providence, sitting on the same hill with the best art and design school in the country, and his son found something obscure and far away instead.

Respecting his mother's request to call his father on his birthday at least, Peter picked up the phone and dialed home. Jockeying the call home hadn't been the same since his parents had split up. There was no Mom to buffer the silences between them. No one to pass the phone to.

"Hello?"

"It's Peter."

"Well, hello. How the hell are you?"

"Fine, I guess. Starting a new class this week. Busy, busy, busy."

"That right? So, what *is* busy, for an artist?" John smiled like it hurt. Peter could hear the smile, the angles of the mouth drawn up and held there.

"It's strange. You wouldn't think art is such hard work, but it is physically exhausting."

"Yeah, you've never been all that physical," John said. "you must get tired easy."

"I'm physical all the time now. It's hard work, which I didn't expect."

"Yeah, your sister is the physical one. You've always been mental," John said.

A pause. "I'm physical," Peter said, "when I want to be."

"Nah," said John. "*Gina* is physical."

"I'm *physical*." Though no one was around to see it, he grabbed a fistful of his shirt fabric, as though assuring himself, at least, of his own physicality.

"Keep it up and you might convince yourself," John said.

"Whatever, Johnny," Peter said, "you know me better than I do, I guess."

"Hold on, now. Don't back away from that. Defend what you said. You made a point: now prove it. What do you do that's physical?" John waited, and the silence on the line dragged.

"No, you're absolutely right, everything you were just saying."

It all came together at once. The indecisiveness, the passivity, and the sheer yieldingness of him. He found it hard to differentiate his flaws from those of his son. It hardly mattered whose, now that Peter was grown.

"You know what the problem with you is, Pete?" John's grimace turned into a pugnacious overbite. "I never smacked you when you were a kid. If I had hit you more, you wouldn't have such a loose fucking attitude."

"Wait a minute," Peter said, letting the anticipation linger. "If *you're* the one who didn't hit me enough, isn't that really a problem with *you*?"

"Don't tempt me. I'm still your father. I'm not above hitting you. I don't care if you *are* twenty fucking years old and living in a loft."

"Okay... so you're gonna fly out to San Francisco and physically beat me?" Peter tried to laugh, but it came out a snort.

"Don't think I won't," said John. He could feel his face go red. He had the look of a tormented boy facing a childhood enemy.

"Okay, Dad, I'll see you in California." He pushed the off-button on his touchtone. On a cordless phone, hanging up the line was so unsatisfying.

This year, the troupe went back and did *Hamlet*. But there were no young volunteers. Richard, at sixty-two years old, had to play the role of Hamlet himself. It was strange at first to see an old man agonizing over his fate, privy to so much doubt, wringing his hands over a simple choice. When a ghost appears in your life and says, "Avenge me," at sixty, you ought to know whether you are going to act on it or not.

Even though she had seen it rehearsed at least twice a week all summer, there was a moment, on opening night, when Abby fell fully under the spell of the play. Before an audience of the King, Hamlet was prompting the players to recite a speech describing the fatal battle between Pyrrhus and Priam, at the height of the siege of Troy, when the peaceful but decadent Trojans, after a decade of war, are finally overrun by the barbarian Achaeans, and their king quartered twice—that is, cut into *eighths*—by Pyrrhus.

The whole production was aimed at unnerving Claudius, the murderer king, upon whom Hamlet was destined to take revenge. But in that moment, before his vengeance could be consummated, *there* was the Prince of Denmark, putting on a *play* to inspire the king's guilt, rather than running him through with his sabre.

Somehow, speaking from his wheelchair gave Richard latent strength—as though, no matter how much passion he put into his performance, he was holding more in reserve.

As the scene ended, Richard spoke in a voice which was simultaneously a yell and a whisper: "The play's the thing / Wherein I'll catch the conscience of the king!"

The performance was so stirring to Abby, she wished for the first time in a long time that her family was all of one piece, if only long enough to watch this play together.

From the window of the plane, John could barely see the peaks and valleys on the surface. The notorious hills of San Francisco seemed barely raised from the rest of the topography, like goosebumps.

On the west coast of America— Peter had said when he first moved there—San Francisco is the closest thing to Providence. He kept referring to its "culture," and the "culture" of Providence, and John couldn't help wondering if he'd meant something other than the local museums. They were both "hip," he'd said, and "progressive." John thought there was something euphemistic about this praise.

As he arrived in the airport lobby—passing, in his first five minutes off the plane, a hare krishna, a thin man with multiple piercings, and what looked like a transvestite—John caught a glimpse into what must be his son's notion of progress.

When he had first moved into the studio, earlier that year, the first thing Peter did was to call his Mom. *He sounds just like a young man*, Abigail thought, as she listened over the phone. Peter couldn't stop talking about the cities he'd lived in. He just couldn't get over the fact of his independence. "That's wonderful, dear," Abigail found herself saying, and thought also of how she must sound just like an old woman.

What he talked about was how kindred their two cities were, yet how different. "San Francisco is, like, a guy who used to write poetry as a teenager, now about to turn thirty, and is looking for something practical—like computers. Providence is this old man who worked in a factory his whole life, who just discovered that there's poetry in him after all."

Abigail had laughed. "I wish there were more men like that. Then we wouldn't have any problems casting for this play."

There was no doorman, no gate, no locks on the door, even.

The studio was wide open, to let in the less-stale air of the hallway. Peter shared the place with two roommates, both of whom were sitting on the couch while Peter shook around in front of them like a fool. They were playing charades, and from John's vantage all the gesturing looked like a mating dance.

Peter looked up, and they briefly made eye contact. John had a lot of expectations: that his son would fight back; that his son would win; that the father would slink off back to Rhode Island like an aging lion. That, maybe, Peter would placate him. What he did not expect was the look of utter surprise on Peter's face. It did not seem possible to him, after twenty years of being a child in his father's house, that Peter would still doubt his word.

As he pulled back for the punch, John swallowed a morsel of air that felt like a hard candy that had gone down by accident. He used this choking sensation to drive his momentum. There was an instant, so brief that it seemed to contain no time at all, that John could have softened the blow. But at that point, what was there to do? At the very least, he wanted his son to be proud of his strength. He followed through with the shot, connecting at the jawline, and sent Peter cringing to the ground— dazed, bruised, and half-coiled up on the floor. He raised his hands to cover his face. He shook his head from side to side. He continued to speak in gestures.

The flight home was faster—blurry, less sequential—more like a montage, as John fluttered in and out of awareness of his surroundings. He looked out of the window; there was no view at night. There was something uneasy about the plane. A lot of missing seats, which meant travellers were staying home instead— had changed plans, had decided not to fly, even after paying for tickets. John stared at all the empty seats wondering, "Who? Who would ever do such a stupid thing?"

Obedient is Mum

August 10, 2006

        In drought
           but green
              no wind   the leaves
   are dry   but dear

     hieroglyphic
hum

in hills and down
                            the lake
   to lip
       whose rings have turned my finger green

A Small Birth There

I

The morning three boys. Each a stumbling
wave of cotton across open acres—
spanning a rise, Spring.

If the morning is a cataract, gazing skyward.
So shapeless children, the vision. Well then the wet field's
push against waking backs.

II

While morning : three boys, beating the holy crap
out of a truck, free of its panicked birds. Weeds
teethe in the wells, the fenders
—nests unbraiding in the belts.

Blameless rituals whose loose time
rises to the ringing : the water-logged bats
and gray axes. The sharded spray—

His mother leans on widow-room appliances,
rubs her chest. Her blank stare calls down rain.
Murmurs over the welts the holes
echo, risen swollen within the fabric.

III

I'm not going to cry all the time.
But open books sow one through the
surrounding copse like silence before
shots. Reports. Stones, small wars

sewing the rivercurves tight to
a rock oxbow : the curling bone of a
wave, still threatening its tidal shadows.

In the setting shade the skin gave way
across grass—evening rose
as did afternoon : from some womb to likewise
walk, talk then crawl up into itself.

Neighbors' woodsmoke rising, fading
into a lake just above the head.

    IV

One pulling seaweed from his mouth.
Another, his body armor-plated
and a red field without cloud or clock. The last boy

found dead in the bighouse attic.
Young hay bending in running step around
his two blue-eyed sisters. Hands in hands,
and what's left.

The girls are muscled barn cats, their musky
lips—everyone touched them. It's fully night,

and what's left of clothing resembles fireflies,
fornicating in the embarrassed trees.
The warm rocks,
the cold river.

    V

So, days ending with them, or us. Or me—
knotted, their arms, legs muddy from the earth
risen from its grave, from the low
country erasing. Some spine, some encased

hope of a fossil, eroded from itself by wind
like drunk fishermen. Crib of sliprocks
in the near and far current, cooing.

Gone under : grazing gestures, naked
in the river. Eddying : young bodies
deposited, sealed to the edgeless stone.

Or wet sounds within the moving wood,
its back turned toward the fading.
And penciled-in birds across
the scene, settling to dusk. To bone.

Hunt

One returned again
and again, slashed against the gray
fences. Rewires

the rust of seasons in the hair.
Over reflective eyes.

Always and always al-
one : tangent trespassing
                a whistling—
sniffs the deeper black
leaves and rain—but fades
in a husked barn. Seems to fall
upwards, something more than snaking
water—hinge, corrugated wind.

                Underboard, a huff amongst shades.
                     His are road-like features :
        part moonshiner knowing best when
     the silver storms' calendars
    from the tail to over temple
—run, run down from the thunderous
You are the riverfires, steaming.

There isn't a lot to add to that
                Virginia, the sun—snuffed—
falling like a slashed palm outward.

If there is no scar, there is
no child   *let there be no child*
Or let the scar be these thunder-headed wombs :
too distant to know
Or the ridges now black
around the silvering shadow

If all this must be new land every so often : it is
filled with the ghosts we'd killed centuries
ago. As the fields' thoughts of river-
stone. As the convict rivers, joke of forgotten
stumpsongs and liars' legends.

One can, walking,
awoke here, a doe
running naked in the breaks. Or simply
           a rosary of lawns. The neighbors,
the neighbors and their frigged
windows

                        Seen at evening : home again,
                             where everyone remembers
        Home again, where the lakefish
wouldn't buy your corpse.

So your long outlines, your spine—
go and end it on a pine, in the arms
of a yellow
dusk. Wet. Winter's teeth within the
sinew—spendthrift.

Get gone upon the roads :
That season's now two counties off,
and now, never coming   the trees
receiving and receiving a sky

and a dimmer ciel, and a night
of scarbeaked birds of prey. Circle and
circling—born of the blood of that one sweating
tree. Only red light along a smooth,

dry fence.
And vision,
spiraling in stasis,
        did roam

Worsen

the cossack vladivostok
comrades dance entrenches

shoot & cover crepitus

rush in mine
pins afore there a farther pull
& toss grenade (fodder
to pinprick)

the why are why our
barbed, raise raze heard
sniper-sharp in straightness
this of punk chirred sandbags
such drabness amidst danger

rife, all pilfered, a steel gun stolen
off a still soldier clicks
& clangs against   canteen
lead a packhorse past
all weak's meat

jaundiced & rotten sons sans,
gang green, cough &
through piss puss in shit
crepitus warble (that crypt)

cigarette tips lit   trace or, torch
you're in crepitus crepitus
pray   come the waves

per flame, per fume
on retreat, we take care to,
debt innate   are ours & all
& temples shot

Child Not Made

when
will it have been
enough, my blood
that for you

rises
        like a swell on the sea
        cresting collapsing
                cubic darkness
                shot with light

rises
        like spiked hackles standing
        at shoulders of dogs on the hunt
                ranging
                ineffable hunger

rises
        like red throats' trumpeting
        from forest beyond the night window,

when:
sated, bodied, of
my blood risen:
you voracious
becoming.

Naming

until that day,
i'd known dislocation, [1]
entirety of dislocation, once [2]

when i'd realized there was a word [3]
for what you had been doing to me. [4]

this time the word [5]

was I, [6]
was I. [7]

---

[1] tasting the blood and the warning of the bird
[2] with no clear perception of the bearing this would have.

[3] a debt engaged in solemn runes on the shaft of a spear
[4] (if anything is unholy it is the oath).

[5] the bird hovers for a while, teasingly

[6] sick of soul
[7] spear once wounded.

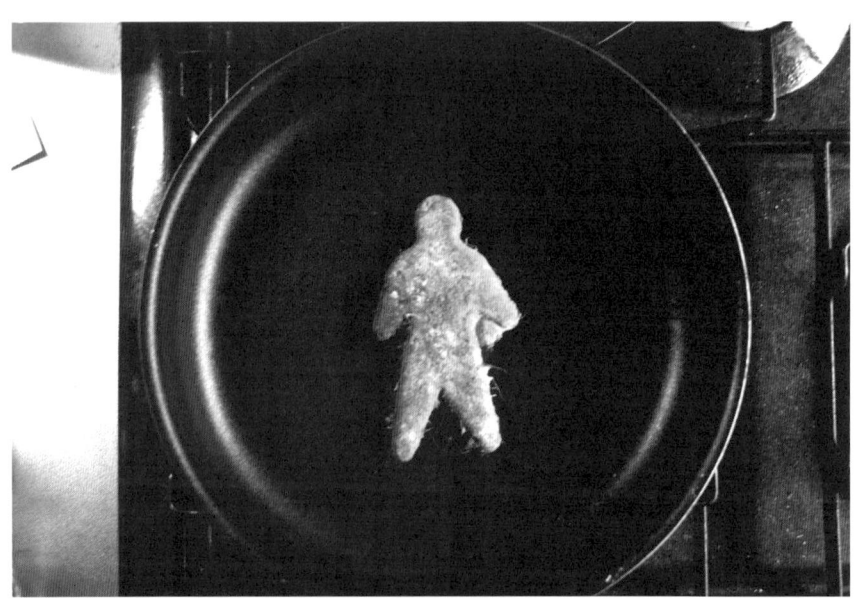

"And That is Life"
-*Russell Peagler*

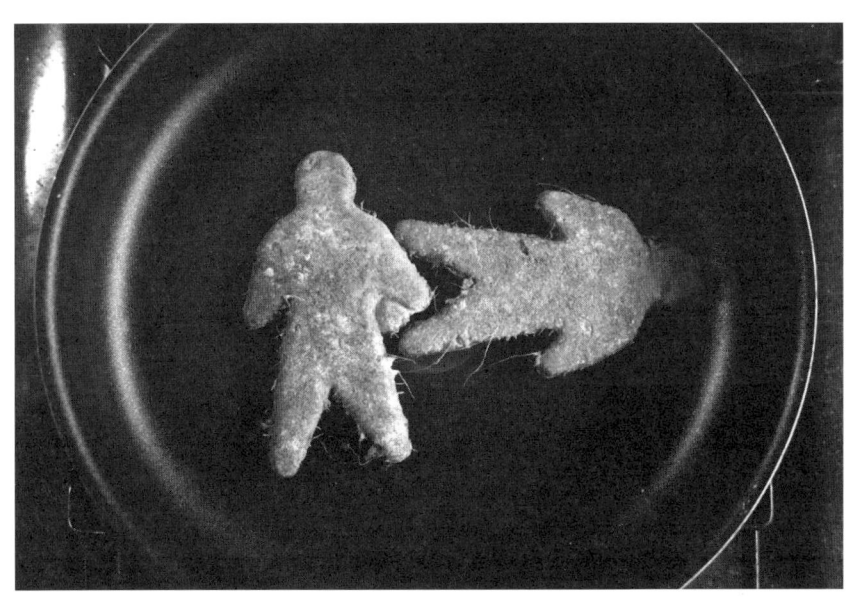

"And That is Life—The Couple"
-*Russell Peagler*

Law of Parsimony

As I have studied science,
I have studied men, and loved them also—
   my cursory diligence, abstracted tenderness:
     in the morning, wake to heresy or sorrow.

It takes me awhile, being back in the world again:
     longings unspooled and artfully rethreaded

It takes me awhile to remember even *this* is optional

But what I admire—
what fetches me time and again to the laboratories
   and the ball fields and the solitary morning strolls
   of Man and Dog or Man with Coffee in Hand and Dog

 is the aspiration of both disciples and discipline:
     the science of men, the men of science:
        toward simplicity, precision.

It takes me awhile to remember that mating is no longer required

And I think of the beauty pageant
     when I was only thirteen, of my mother winding
       my hair over hot rollers' sticky spikes
       my body shrinking right before our eyes
        That was Ockham's Razor also

shaving my legs until, bare and bony, they bled
     stripping the hair away from my under-arms
       and the tender tops of my toes

Turning sallow then, my breath tucked in,
   Vaselined teeth and yellowing nails: cut down to size
     pink lace and white ruffles cuffing me tight

       scrutiny of a Marriott's worth of strangers
         That was Ockham's Razor also

It takes me awhile to let the tears drain out of my lungs:
   to breathe again: alive and exonerated

And I think of how it really did look simple on paper:
   a marriage license for sixty bucks and bumming
   a cigarette from the city worker watching the door

"What'd ya want to get married for?"
     with his scruffy chin and his pretty eyes and his patience,
       waiting for me to reply

A slew of answers:
   Because it's easier to vote the party line
   Because even cable is never a la carte
   Because I'm a writer: I understand about sentences,
     dependent clauses, conditional and subordinate terms
  And because I have memorized precisely what I am supposed to want
    (They don't call it a steel trap for nothin')

Something about parents and needing to please them, or defy them;
   something about safety and needing to seek it at all costs;
     something about other people understanding that I had been wanted,
       and sought after, and heartily desired

It takes me awhile to remember, under penalty of perjury, the old Natural Law

What can be said of the beloved: percussion of her body's praise, deep
   mysterious music that undergirds these syllables but cannot be translated
     into speech: syncopation, improvisation…

And what can be said of the world, with its bristles and Brill-o pads and either/or boxes: that the simplest answer is always the best? that accuracy can be calculated, quantified and contained?

What then of desire's capacity to surprise us, of the improbable majesty of the willow-tree and the comforting disquietude of the storm?

The science is impersonal, without eyes. The men are lovely sometimes, but trained the way snipers stalk through the wild: a single target in a circular outline: circumference no greater than a dime…*bull's eye*

It takes me awhile: to collect myself and my follies and the ivy-twined inquiries of my mind.

It takes me awhile.   She knows this.   In her own intricacy: unabashed and labyrinthine: she sees.

THE WINDMILLS OF ALTAMONT PASS

The hills are the hulls of upside down boats;
The rotations sprinkler the vineyard:

Herb garden, wine press, fishbones.
Canary date palms spread like an idea of

The rotations: *Sprinkler.* The vineyard's
Tractor tires, now gardens, now sandboxes.

Canary date palms spread like an idea of
An idea about artichokes, and the fields'

Tractor tires, now harvested gardens. Sandboxes
At the center, small castles, their spires--

An idea about artichokes. And the fields
Arc wide under foothills of wine country,

At the center, small castles. Their spires
Oversee the meandering vines, a view

Arcing wide over foothills of wine country,
The lake's speedboat, the docks' moor

Oversea, other meandering vines, a view,
Over watershed, from wine press, a propeller,

Another speedboat. The dock is more
Concerned with not being a bridge

Over watershed. From a wine press, propellers
Churn black bass into Cabernet.

Concerned with not being a bridge
Between here and there, hill and air,

Turning black bass into Cabernet--
Falling Angels? Samaras.

The hills are hulls of upside down boats:
The windmills of Altamont Pass.
Herb garden, wine press, fishbones.

[Crease in the field of morning]

Crease in the field of morning
Thought scatters through stalks of grain
Lavender limestone sawdust
The sun fails to speak
Melting snow erodes enclosures
Blocking songs' progress into town
Sheep gather on the edge of the field
Stamping patterns into the earth
Each image spurns memory and
We tuck snapshots away
Preferring not to make them our own
Ribbons deck daily guarantees
Promenade across existence
Offers by old arrangements

Broken Tulip

blushed, i bartered his horticultry
(i wanted so bad to be that sophisticated type)

give me two, will you –
i'll be more expensive, i said in my lazy
bulb head, *cultivate me with a name.*

he juiced the soil as i squinted complete.

& i felt the colors rush,
as he sewed sweetmeat coins to my feet
& sketched the wings of me tucked up.

read: the invention of the both-flower.

in the morning i broke of dirtsugar and lake,
& found his prayers pressed on my bloodface

store me, i said
in a dark and not damp place
adore me with your coldish,

i'll be this one-day discovery of yours, if you
also at my stem.

Like Gods of the Sun

The thermometer on the wall of the pool locker room reads an improbable 107 degrees Fahrenheit, as it has now for four days running. It is two-fifteen in the afternoon; the Midwestern sun is high and orange and the sky is a gun-metal blue. The pool smells less of chlorine than of damp, heated asphalt. From the proper angle the blacktop of the parking lot looks like a vast, shimmering ocean. At last count, there are one-hundred-and-thirty-two people in and around the pool.

Baumeier, the manager on duty here, opens the door to the office and peaks out over the deck. He glances up at the clock and lets out a low curse. Fifteen minutes left on his shift and he is done. Finished. This is his last day on the job. The sun and constant heat make his head pound; his mouth tastes like an oily rag. He passed the night on a stranger's couch and has not yet showered. Come Monday, he will be sitting in an air-conditioned cubicle, far away from all this adolescent foolishness. He steps free of the office, head down; the gold flash of a whistle spins absently around an outstretched finger. He runs his other hand through his hair, and catches wind of a familiar scent, something slightly sour and foreign and somehow—off.

Teenagers, burnished copper from the August sun, snap towels at the curves of exposed thighs and dodge shrieking in and out of the locker rooms. Wrinkled, prune-like children skitter across the pool deck from the diving board to the slide and back again, their dark footprints disappearing from the glistening pool deck moments after they pass. Above all of this, ensconced on high at regular intervals around the pool, are several figures clad in red swim shorts and white t-shirts. From a distance they appear bright and featureless, as if they might melt or burst into flame without warning.

Baumeier does not see any of this; he hurries back into the shadows of the men's locker room to wash his hands and fetch out another bag of ice.

***

One of the aforementioned wrinkled, prune-like children is three-and-a-half-year-old Myra. She is red-headed and freckled and is often told she is "smart beyond her years." She does not really know what this means, not yet, but she knows enough to blush when she is complimented. Myra holds a bright red novelty drink which she has just purchased for forty cents from the snack bar. The novelty drink is in a tiny plastic container shaped like a barrel, and it has drawn the attention of two wasps who have tracked her progress from the snack bar to her corner of the shallow end. Myra cups a hand over the mouth of the drink and bounces up and down on the balls of her feet. She sneaks a sip from the container and the wasps break formation for a moment only to return again in earnest. One of the wasps pauses by her ear, buzzing frantically as if to whisper some final taunt, as if to say *That is mine, give it to me,* and then she is in the pool with a fearful shriek. She bobs underwater for the briefest of moments and then is buoyed by orange water-wings. In a blind panic she paddles over to her mother, a large woman floating idly on a blue raft; a moment later she is playing London Bridges Falling Down with some other children. The novelty drink lies forgotten on the pool deck, consumed quickly by the wasps and the fat, slow sun.

***

Hernandez emerges from the main building and holds up a single, well-manicured hand to shade his eyes. After the darkness and reprocessed air of the facility the sun comes as a blind shock. He is sixty-two years old, wears plaid swimming trunks and has a white health club towel slung over his left shoulder. He has a large golden ring on each hand, a gold imitation Rolex on his wrist and a bright St. Christopher medal around his neck. From a distance, he looks like some forgotten conquistador emerged from the galley of his ship to survey a new land.

Since his retirement in June, he has spent most of his time at community centers like this one. He does not swim, but he enjoys the bustle of bright, flawless bodies moving across the deck. He has been a member of three different pool clubs in as many months. Things ended badly at the last place; there was talk of expulsion and, possibly, police involvement.

Hernandez walks to the shallow end, greeting a familiar face here and there along the way. He is not in any particular hurry. He sits down by the edge of the pool in the shadow of an empty lifeguard stand and lays his towel over the top rung of the ladder.

Something has changed in Hernandez these past few weeks, something other than just the specifics of his everyday routine. It is almost as though a wire has come loose somewhere in the dark spaces of his mind, snapping like a downed power line. His dreams come hot and confused, full of moist, soft curves and pistoning bodies. His waking thoughts are more of the same:

tangled, damp. He finds himself constantly distracted and unable to focus on the simplest of tasks. It is almost, he thinks, as though he's going through a second puberty. His wife has remarked on this several times recently, his new-found "interest" as she calls it, and he takes it as something of a point of honor. None of those ridiculous potency drugs for him.

What he is about to do, however, has no discernable sexual component whatsoever. It seems to him as ordinary and necessary as relieving himself. True, there is always a young, female lifeguard within sight, but this seems only a small piece of the composite experience. The lifeguard across from him—young, petite, brunette—has not even glanced at him. He could be anyone from anywhere; he is an old man; he is nobody. As he watches, she tucks her sunburned knees up under her t-shirt, takes a sip of water.

Hernandez lifts his arms over his head and stretches. Then, with a deft, subtle movement of his left hand, he lifts the leg of his swim trunks and exposes himself.

Hernandez looks about quickly, to make sure no one has marked his presence, then leans back to enjoy the bright August sun.

***

Caroline is up in the lifeguard stand by the shallow end, the one the guards refer to as Number Six. She's having what is, in her own words, one shit-banger of a day. The previous evening they'd thrown a surprise party for Baumeier, one of the pool managers, and her head still pounds from the ensuing hangover. The party was for his "retirement"; he'd recently graduated from college and landed a cake job at a local accounting firm. There is a bottle of Aquafina between Caroline's feet which she sips from occasionally, but it's doing little to clear the cotton from her mouth and the fuzz from her brain.

She has been sixteen for two months now and this is her first job. She is concerned that her behavior at the party was something of an embarrassment. She remembers having a few glasses of some humorously named drink (Sex on the Beach? Strip-and-Go-Naked?); she remembers music, bodies jostling against one another in a narrow kitchen. The only other recollection she has is of a brief semi-romantic interlude with one of the other guards, and—here is the chief source of her embarrassment—she can't quite remember which one. The rest is a thick, vague darkness.

She takes a drink of the water and tries to focus her attention on the pool. A blue raft has drifted into the shallow end, and on top is one of the largest women she's ever seen. The woman is reading what appears to be a paperback romance novel. A pretty little red-haired girl, the woman's daughter, is trying her best to dive down underneath the raft despite the half-inflated floaties on her arms. Caroline recognizes the girl from one of her swim classes, but can't remember her name. She's a fantastic little swimmer, a veritable fish, and has the kick of a kid twice her age. She remembers the mother, too—Sue Beth or Sue Ann or something—a bloated, overprotective bear of a woman who is constantly interfering with her swim lessons.

"Don't hold your nose!" Caroline calls, "Kick!" but the little girl is not listening. The raft—one of those thick, expensive air mattresses, not the dime-store junk—does not belong in the shallow end. But in lifeguarding, as in life, there are rules and there are Rules, as she's fast beginning to figure out. No diving head first into the shallow end is a Rule. No rafts in the shallow end, well, that's something of a gray area.

She feels something cold against the back of her leg, and when she looks down sees Baumeier standing below. "Hey hey," he says. Baumeier has this manner of standing when he's on duty that is at once annoyingly formal and oddly reassuring. He never looks up at whomever he's speaking to, but always out over the water. He's holding a bucket filled with ice water and cut up pieces of towels. He hands one up to her. "Put this over the back of your neck," he says.

"Where's that storm you promised," says Caroline.

Baumeier removes his sunglasses for a moment and looks up at the sky. To the lay-person it could seem empty, as blank as slate. There are striations up there in the atmosphere, however, imperfections on the western horizon.

"It's coming. You sure you're alright?"

"I told you I'm fine." Even as she says this, she feels a new wave of nausea run from somewhere deep in her stomach up to her throat. She peeks down at Baumeier to see if he's as hungover as he's claimed, but he appears the same as always. She takes some small confidence from this and is glad he's on today rather than that bitch Leslie. Everyone has told her that if she'd just throw up she'd probably feel better. She was doubtful of the wisdom before, but now she's not so sure. "Maybe if I can have, like, a twenty-minute break on this next rotation—" she says.

But Baumeier is not listening. He is peering down into the water right in front of stand Number Six. "Son of a bitch," he says.

"What's wrong now?" she asks, but as soon as she looks down, she sees exactly what's wrong. A cluster of child-size feces floats peacefully in the water beneath her stand. As she watches, the currents of the pool begin to scatter them off to parts unknown.

"You've got to be shitting me," Baumeier hisses. "That little son of a *bitch*." When he looks back up at Caroline his expression has darkened, and she is suddenly afraid. "Listen. Get that fucking raft out of the shallows. And keep an eye on Pat over there in the deep end, he's acting funny. I'll be right back."

Caroline has never seen Baumeier like this.

She sits up and puts her whistle to her lips, more alert now than she's been all day. She's about to get raft woman's attention when she notices something new. There's a gentleman sitting across the shallow end by the edge of the pool—he looks strangely exotic, Spanish maybe. His legs are slightly akimbo, and he's holding something in his hand. Caroline lowers her whistle slowly, and both the raft and its passenger are forgotten. She knows what it is the guy is holding, in theory at least, if not in practice.

"That's a cock," she says, and makes a sound that is part laughter and part something else. "Baumeier. Hey, I think you better—!" she calls, but he has already disappeared into the men's locker room.

***

Baumeier is in the blackest of moods. It is 2:19 pm, his last day on the job, eleven minutes before the end of his shift, and that little bastard has to pop a squat in his pool. The shit itself is not the issue; that can be left for the next shift, after all. It's the principle of the thing. The excrement, wandering around the shallows like a school of little brown crappie, seems, in his current mood, like some sort of personal slight. Worse yet, the new guy who is supposed to relieve him hasn't shown yet. He was supposed to be in at two o'clock, so Baumeier could go over a few last-minute details. Baumeier opened the pool at 6:30 this morning and has been on duty ever since. In that time he has been ill twice, out back behind the supply closet.

Now he has his prime suspect cornered in the locker room back by the urinals. "Listen," Baumeier says again. "Did you crap in my pool?" The kid is one of those so-called Special Needs kids and his name is Rich or Rick or something, and he's clearly not paying Baumeier any mind.

"I already told you, he doesn't understand." Rich's keeper, one of the counselors, is standing behind him. She knows better than this. Baumeier personally handed each one of the counselors a memo on the health risks of excrement in a public pool. All campers, special or not, are supposed to defecate before they swim, not during. As if reading his mind, she says, "Look, I can't just make him poop, you know."

"Like hell you can't."

The counselor's name is Bobbie or Billie or something. They knew one another back in school, made out once in the bleachers during a football game. He has since forgotten her name, and she his. She is not supposed to be in the men's locker room, of course, but they've had that conversation before. Baumeier's attention is now focused wholly on Rich.

"Oh. Okay, Baum—whatever your name is," she's saying now. "You're right, I must have left my do-it-yourself enema kit out in the car."

Baumeier looks up; he's not sure if it's the sarcasm or her casual, opportune usage of the word *enema,* but he suddenly finds her oddly attractive. "Hey," he says, backpedaling now. "Am I the asshole here? I've got 270,000 gallons of turd soup out there, and now I'm the asshole. Fine. Just great." He leans down so his face is just inches from Rich's nose. A piece of wet toilet paper dangles from the kid's chin. "But, oh," he says, "I've got my eye on you, kiddo." With this, Baumeier turns and stalks out of the locker room to go see what in God's name Pat is up to. His head throbs, and he begins to think he might need to head out to the supply closet for another go.

***

Up on top of the high dive, Kristin gets ready for another try. She has been off the high dive countless times in her life, but this is the first time she is going to attempt a flip. There is more of a breeze from this vantage point, and the air is balmy and pleasant. Everything possesses a kind of bright clarity up here. She is keenly aware of every sensation—the wetness of the board, the hard, rough granules pressing up beneath her feet. Today is her thirteenth birthday, and her present from her parents is a week's stay at Space Camp down in Florida. The real deal. She's wanted this for as long as she can remember. She imagines that the push of the diving board—the sudden pressure and then that breathless moment of weightlessness—is something like going into space.

Kristin begins her count back from ten. *10-9-8—* Not out loud, of course, but in her head.

She tunes out everything around her, the breeze, the feel of the board, everything but the lifeguard below her calling up encouragement. *Let's go, baby! Make this one pop!* he shouts. Kristin has been trying to catch his attention all summer to no avail. She wears her cutest bikini, walks underneath his guard stand five, six times in an afternoon. His name is Pat. Patrick—an Irish name, her sister says, but she thinks it's cute. Now all of a sudden, he's right there under the board, cheering her every dive. When Kristin asks her sister what she should do, she always grunts and tells her to "get his number." She's not sure what she would do with Pat's number even if he'd give it to her, but she's decided that if she nails the flip she's going to ask him anyway. Kristin can see her sister just across the pool chatting with some friends by the shallow end. She waves to her, but her sister isn't looking.

—*6-5-4 (Ignition!) 3-2*— And then she's off. She takes her last few steps, feels the reassuring thrust of the board, and then she's airborne. Something is off though, right from the get go. Somewhere between those last few steps and her movement into the rotation she notices something out of place, off to her left, not more than thirty feet away, down by the shallow end of the pool. There's a man down there holding something that's probably best left un-held. And isn't there something a little spooky about the gesture, maybe even a little threatening? She tries to correct herself, to make the necessary adjustments, but her arm is now flung wide and her legs are back over her head. *Houston, we have a prob*— And then there's nothing, save for water in her mouth and nose and static in her ears.

***

Under the surface of the water, everything is quiet and at peace. Myra has discovered that if she works her water-wings down to her forearms, she can jimmy her way under the raft hands first. Arms, head, and then a few well-timed kicks just like her swim instructor taught her, and—*pop*—she's in. There's a moment of sweet and terrible womb-like stasis, a great protective silence unlike anything else she can imagine. She pauses there for a moment, as if on the dark side of a vast, blue planet. She can see the light of the sun off in the distance, rising as she moves closer. Then there is another *pop* and she slides out on the other side, the force of the raft's weight coasting her almost to the wall. She floats there for a moment in the pool like a waterlogged Raggedy Ann doll, and then sits up, giggling. She turns herself around and then swims back to the raft to start the whole process again. Her mother pats her head and returns to her book.

***

As he exits the locker room, Baumeier notices Caroline trying to get his attention. They've worked together quite a bit this summer and have established a pretty good rapport. When he sees her hand waving, he knows it is not out of panic or imminent disaster—it's not the Big One as they sometimes say—but rather a matter that requires subtlety and some degree of urgency. If disaster were imminent, Carline would be standing, blowing her whistle loud enough to rouse the entire neighborhood.

Baumeier walks over in the direction she's pointing. He finds nothing out of the ordinary, just an older gentleman sitting under an empty guard stand. He's leaning back with his eyes closed, enjoying the sun, and Baumeier steps up behind him quietly. A health club towel hangs on the top rung of the ladder. Caroline is pointing now, frantically, straight at him, but nothing seems out of place. It seems, in fact, as if the area has mostly cleared out around this man.

"Excuse me, sir," Baumeier says. "Are you using this towel?" He's scanning the area, looking out over the water, trying to figure out the source of Caroline's distress. He glances down quickly into the man's face and then back out over the shallows.

The gentleman opens his eyes slowly, as if waking from a long dream. When he speaks the movements of his mouth don't quite match up with his words, as if he is speaking from a great distance. "That is ridiculous," the man says quietly.

There is something both foreign and odd in this man's manner of speech. Something off, but *(that is ridiculous)* he can't seem to put his finger on it. "The towel," says Baumeier. "Health club towels are supposed to stay inside. We have other towels for your use here at the pool."

The grating sound of the man's voice makes the throbbing in Baumeier's head increase ten-fold. "But I am not wet, you see. Why would I need a towel?"

Baumeier takes the towel from the top rung of the ladder. "I apologize for disturbing you," he says. He takes one last look around the shallow end. The blue raft is still there—at least that little girl is no longer trying to burrow her way underneath. Caroline is no longer pointing at him, but glaring with sullen disappointment. Baumeier points at the raft and pantomimes blowing his whistle. Caroline holds up her right hand and slowly, inexplicably, extends her middle finger. He considers doing it himself, but why give her the satisfaction? It is 2:26, he has four minutes left on his shift, and high, thick clouds are beginning to pass in front of the sun. He heads off again in search of Pat.

***

Pat is on break, at least technically speaking. He watches as an older woman dives gracefully off the high dive. The entire process is fascinating. She arches forward gracefully, muscles taut, waiting for that perfect moment when conscious effort ceases and gravity takes over. She falls for several long moments and then the water swallows her up, sending particles of blue liquid up into the atmosphere like thousands of cold, glimmering stars.

Usually he sits in the guard lounge on his break, smokes a cigarette, eats a granola bar—but today he has far too much energy. Pat is starting to think he has made a terrible error in judgment. This morning, during a particularly onerous brunch with his jerk-off father, Pat decided to drop a tab and a half of acid, just to take the edge off. The acid is not the problem; he has already pretty much decided that this is quite possibly the best decision he's ever made. The problem is that a few moments previous he made the mistake of confiding his altered state to Jerry. Jerry is at least twice his age and, by all accounts, a very cool cat. Pat figured if anyone would be sympathetic to his current state of mind, Jerry would. Instead, Jerry is sitting sullenly up in guard stand Number Three, probably deciding whether or not to rat him out.

Pat keeps trying to make small talk, but apparently he and Jerry are no longer on speaking terms. He tries to tell Jerry that he's on his way down—e.t.a. 3:30 at the latest—that he's just arrived at that place when the trip, like some great tidal wave of synapses and neurons, is about to crest and roll back upon itself. Jerry does not answer, however, and there's no sense in worrying about it now.

More important than any of this, Pat has discovered a new mental talent. He's figured out that if he concentrates at just the right moment, he can make girls' bikini tops pop off as they hit the water. Four out of seven tries is just too uncanny to be coincidence.

Pat watches as a girl makes her way to the end of the board. He recognizes her; she's no more than thirteen and has been giving him the eye all afternoon. Krista or Kristin, he thinks her name is. She had a pretty rough landing on her last dive and the top part of her chest is an angry red. A real trooper. "C'mon," he says. "Let's see that two-and-a-half gainer, baby."

She peers down at him, blushing. "You might want to go take a look at that guy over there. He's sitting funny and it's kind of creepy," Kristin says.

"Let's just get this show on the road, eh?" Pat claps his hands and raises his arms in the air as if to do the wave. "C'mon, big money! *Make it pop!*"

***

Jerry has come to a difficult decision regarding Pat. In his long life he has done many unconscionable things, most of which he will admit to in great detail if you ask him. Back in the sixties and seventies he was a pilot for Eastern. They kept a tight schedule, worked hard and played hard. There had been many times when he'd taken the control stick with the taste of the previous night's indiscretion lingering on his tongue, burning in his nose. If asked, he will tell you he's seen the inside of every airport cocktail lounge in the continental United States. Those were different times, certainly, but what about that landing at Metcalf, when the runway lights melted into so many millions of white hot droplets, each with its own keening voice? And nothing had ever gone bad, not really, not on his watch. But if he's learned anything in his time, it's that there is a difference between providence and dumb luck.

Baumeier rounds the corner of the diving well, moving fast, his eyes fixed on Pat. As he passes stand Number Three, Jerry calls out. "Baumeier, if I could have a word—"

***

Underneath the raft, everything is dark and growing darker. A deep, depthless, twilight blue. Something went wrong on that last pass. The thin sunrise that greeted Myra on each of her last few orbits has failed to appear, her left floatie snagged now on some object unseen. She is stuck; frightened but not yet terrified. She flips herself over to get a better view. There are grooves in the bottom of the air mattress and Myra presses her face into these now, taking in thin gasps of air. *Mom,* she says, but no sound comes out, just a thin, rubbery echo. *Mom—*

***

Although she is doing her best to keep it under control, Caroline's gorge is definitely on the rise. She takes a sip from her water bottle and leans forward. He's still over there, that nasty old man, waggling his dong at her. Look at him. Sitting back, eyes closed, just another day down at the pool. His wrinkled, purple, old man penis hangs loose from the leg of his plaid swimming trunks. At first it was amusing, almost.

The area around the man has cleared out as if by some tacit agreement. Once, an old lady walked out of the locker room stark naked and just stood there, confused. People averted their eyes, continued their business around her as if she were possessed of a strange, ill-defined contagion.

Worse yet, Caroline's exploits from the previous evening are beginning to come back to her. She remembers a strange bed in a strange house.

A stranger's hand has worked its way down the front of her pants. *Inside of her*, she thinks, the phrase feeling strange and alien and somehow wrong. The room is dark save for the occasional glare of headlights from a passing car, and her hips are moving as if of their own volition, in time to the music, her hands gripping the backboard of the bed which rattles rhythmically against the wall, and she has a driving urge to giggle.

And over all of this looms the veined specter of that old man's cock, like some cheap, misshapen special effect in a bad late-night horror flick. Baumeier, that motherfucker.

She is trapped up here. She feels like a piece of meat on a hook left to hang in a very high place. A high, tight fluttering rises in her chest. If she doesn't get down soon, she's not sure what might happen.

"Excuse me miss, are you alright?" A young, handsome father is standing next to her now, looking up with concern. "You look kind of—green."

Caroline bends over so her face is right next to his and enunciates each word carefully. "*How, could, he, not, fuck, ing, see, it?*"

***

Baumeier's mood has improved substantially over the past few moments. Two minutes left. And he's never liked Pat, has looked for an excuse to get rid of him ever since he first darkened his doorway. He thanks Jerry and continues around the pool.

"Hey hey, Bummeister," Pat says.

Pat knows he's busted, Baumeier can hear it in the kid's voice. "I've been meaning to have a talk with you regarding Professionalism in the Workplace," says Baumeier, grinning widely now. "Shifting Career Strategies in a Post-Boom Economy. Things of that nature."

"Yeah, sure. Whatever, man."

"First, however, I have a little job for you. I need you to go over to the supply closet and get out the vacuum. We've had a little accident over in the shallow end, and I need you to clean it up. You remember the vacuum, right? Big, cumbersome, cylindrical thing, long tube, long pole? Used for sucking up shit?" Baumeier's face looks like it could split open at any moment.

"Yeah, man. I'm flying the friendly skies here, Bummeister," says Pat. "Not retarded."

Pat turns to head over to the supply closet and then stops. "Hey, Bummeister," he says. "Check this out." Pat closes his eyes and holds his hand up towards the high dive. There is a woman up there now, mid-twenties, attractive. The woman bounces once, falls for a few long moments and then slips into the water. Perfect form.

"That's great, Pat—"

"Keep watching."

There is nothing down there but froth on the water and the woman's shadow, first touching bottom and then angling towards the ladder. Then, as if out of nowhere, a pair of red white and blue bikini bottoms floats up to the surface of the pool.

"Un-fucking-canny," says Pat, and continues on his way.

***

Pat rounds the corner of the shallow end, enroute to the supply closet. He's moving quickly now; he knows he's finished here, wants to get it over with, wants to just do the thing and be done with it. As he passes stand number five, he sees a man sitting by himself. His legs are open and his family jewels—the royal scepter, the whole package—are hanging loose for anyone to see.

"Whoa," says Pat. "Better slap some SPF #30 on that puppy."

He walks on, but there is definitely a bad vibe down in this corner of the universe. A *bad mojo*, as Jerry likes to say. The area is mostly empty, save for a woman on a blue raft reading a trashy novel, *The Wives of Lord Claudius*, or some such foolishness. Caroline is up in Number Six, glaring out towards Baumeier. He looks over in that direction and sees the gold flash of a whistle twirling on Baumeier's finger, clockwise and back again, clockwise and back again. The sun is almost gone now, and a cool breeze is beginning to blow. Something feels off here, yet everything seems in its right place. There is a low rumbling off in the distance, as yet inaudible. Not quite thunder, not yet, but the precursor to thunder. Pat continues on, fast now and moving faster.

***

Lord Claudius pulls Evelyn close to him and gazes in her eyes, searchingly. "I have dreamt of this for a long time," he says.

Evelyn reaches down between his legs. His member presses up against her, a bold exclamation point beneath the fabric of his trousers. She takes him in her hand. "But what would you have me do? Leave William? I too have dreamt—"

Sue Ann lays the book face down in her lap. Seven pages to go. She knows this because she's flipped to the end several times already this afternoon. She's read this particular novel three times and it always gets to her.

She wants to finish it off, but she's losing her sunlight and it's getting late. She glances down at her wrist, and then remembers she left her watch up on the deck, next to her purse. She looks over and sees (*a bold exclamation point*) something—awful.

Sue Ann sits up quickly—*bolts* rather—and turns to get a better look. When she does, there is a low *pop*ping sound beneath her rump.

A small form floats free of the raft.

In a single movement, faster than you might plausibly credit to a woman of her size, she springs free and scoops Myra up in her arms, holds her up to the sky. Her daughter's eyes are wide, lips blue. She shakes her daughter once, twice. When Myra opens her mouth there is a moment of seemingly interminable silence, and then a flood of pinkish-gray liquid pours from her mouth and nose.

Sue Ann turns to the nearest lifeguard stand, but the girl in stand six is not looking at her, is not looking at anything at all. The guard's knees are tucked up under her t-shirt and she stares off into empty space. Sue Ann remembers something (a man) sitting somewhere in the vicinity of the girl's gaze, but now there is nothing, there is no one around at all.

Still holding her daughter to the sky, Sue Ann finds her voice, begins to scream.

***

Baumeier sits in the air-conditioned pool office, an unlit cigarette dangling from his lips. It is 2:31pm. The new guy has finally arrived; his car broke down back on Kellogg Avenue and he had to hump it all the way in, a distance of almost two miles. His shirt is soaked through with sweat. The door is closed and the A/C runs on high; there is no other sound. Aside from the life-saving equipment strewn about the office—backboard, oxygen mask, life buoy—they could be in any office, anywhere.

Baumeier turns to the new guy. "Alright," he says. "Pat's on shit detail; just send him home when he's finished. But keep an eye on him. Make sure the area around the vacuum is clear, and don't let the extension cord touch any stray water along the deck. We don't need another incident like the one in '98. We were fishing out bodies for weeks."

The new guy does not smile at this, does not even twitch.

Baumeier places his left hand on the new guy's face and slaps him playfully with his right. "It's a joke, buddy. Relax. We're having fun here."

Outside the narrow office window the sky has gone gray. Baumeier needs a cigarette, needs to roll up the windows of his car before the storm hits. "I'll be back in a minute," he says, but this feels like a lie. He hands the new guy the keys to the pool.

Baumeier steps out of the office into the parking lot, lights his cigarette, walks to his car. The sun is gone and a cool, balmy breeze has taken its place. He likes this place. He likes the people, likes that they like him. In a week he will be wearing a suit, sitting in a cubicle not much larger than one of the lifeguard stands. In a week this place will seem like any of the other past events in his life, blurred, distant—a dream. He will remember this time in his life fondly, this place, these endless summer days, back before the urgent business of his life had properly begun.

Baumeier's car door is already open, radio on, when he catches sight of a man exiting the locker room, heading toward him. Gold flashes from his neck and wrist and from his fingers in the failing light. The man walks with an air of authority; he could almost be a king or some forgotten conqueror. The man produces a cigarette, asks for a light, and he and Baumeier smoke in companionable silence.

After a while the man turns to Baumeier and says: "This is a good place. I've tried a few others. But this. This is it." He offers Baumeier his hand, and a sudden peel of thunder rumbles on the western horizon.

Baumeier waits for the sound of a lifeguard's whistle—two long blasts to clear the pool. But once the whistle starts it keeps going, five seconds, then ten. Something is wrong. Through the fence he can see Jerry up in stand three, standing now, shading his eyes and peering toward the shallows beyond Baumeier's line of sight. Pat does nothing; he stands in front of the half-assembled vacuum—arms wide, eyes closed—the new wind blowing his hair wild. Baumeier looks at the old man's wrinkled hand, then back toward the pool. There is nothing here out of the ordinary: Jerry on high, gazing into some unseen distance, and Pat, arms thrown wide and smiling up at a graying sky. Everything is perfectly still. For a moment he considers heading back inside, toward the sound of that lone, awful whistle, blowing as if it might never stop.

Instead however he takes the old man's hand, and through his cigarette Baumeier says: "I'm glad to hear that."

Baumeier and the old man glance at each other briefly, and as if by some unspoken accord the old man walks off, Baumeier climbs in his car, slams the door tight. By the time the first sirens sound in the distance Baumeier is already eastbound on the highway, something vague and distant on the radio, a stiff wind at his back.

Contributors

Karen Leona Anderson is a graduate of the University of Iowa's Writers' Workshop and the recipient of a Rotary Scholarship to New Zealand who has had work published in *Jubilat, Verse, Indiana Review, The New Republic, Fence, Volt*, and other journals. She is currently writing a dissertation on poetry and science in Ithaca, New York, where she also helps curate the SOON reading series.

M.D. Baumgartner lives in Las Vegas with his wife, where he is a Schaeffer Fellow in creative writing at the University of Nevada-Las Vegas and the International Institute of Modern Letters. His most recent work has been featured in magazines such as the *Tampa Review* and *Wisconsin Review*. He is currently finalizing a collection of short stories and working on a novel.

James Belflower is a Master's Candidate in Creative Writing at University of Colorado at Boulder. His poetry appeared or is forthcoming from *26, First Intensity, Banyan Review*, and *Square One*, among others. James' awards include: *The Banyan Review* Poetry Competition Finalist, two Jovanavich Awards for his graduate thesis, *Friend of Mies van der Rohe*, and graduate manuscript, *Site*, as well as honorable mention in the Milton Dorfman Poetry competition.

Angus Bennett currently teaches in Austin, TX. He holds an MFA in Poetry from the Iowa Writer's Workshop and is a PhD candidate in Rhetoric at the University of North Carolina Greensboro. His work also appears in the Spring/Summer 2006 issue of the *Alaska Quarterly Review*.

Joelle Biele lives in Ellicot City, MD. She is the author of the book, *White Summer*, which was the winner of the *Crab Orchard Review* First Book Award. Her poems have appeared or are forthcoming in *Crazyhorse, Crab Orchard Review*, and *Gulf Coast*.

John Blair lives in San Marcos, TX, and directs the undergraduate creative writing program at Texas State University. He has published two novels, and his short story collection *American Standard* was the 2002 winner of the Drue Heinz Literature Prize and was published by the *University of Pittsburgh Press*. He has recent stories in *The Sewanee Review, The Antioch Review*, and *The Portland Review*.

Martin Corless-Smith was born and raised in Worcestershire, England. His last book was *Swallows* (Fence Books, NYC). His next is *English Fragments/A Brief History of the Soul* (West House Books, Sheffield, England).

Kurtis Davidson is the penname of Kurt Jose Ayau and David Rachels, who both teach at the Virginia Military Institute. As well as having published a dozen collaborative stories in a variety of magazines, Ayau and Rachels are the authors of an award-winning comic novel, *What the Shadow Told Me*. Download the first chapter for free at: KurtisDavidson.com.

Haines Eason's recent work appears in *Pleiades, Yale Review*, and *Smartish Pace*, among other journals. He lives in San Francisco.

Reba Elliott lives with two friends, one a dog, in Washington, D.C.

Jim Goar teaches at Ewha University in Seoul. His first book, *Whole Milk* (effing press), was published a year ago. His most recent series, *Winter on the 109* (H_angm_n Books), will be published later this year. He edits the online journal, *past simple*.

Georges Godeau was born in 1921 in Villiers-en-Plaine, France, worked as an engineer, and published sixteen books before his death in 1999. His work won the Prix du Livre in Poitou-Charentes. Widely translated into Russian and Japanese, next to none of his work has appeared in English.

Eleanor Graves teaches yoga and meditation in Washington, D.C. She also works for the Education Department of the Freer and Sackler Galleries, the Asian Art Museum of the Smithsonian, teaching poetry workshops to kids and families. Her poems have appeared in *Phoebe, Practice: New Writing + Art*, and *Hayden's Ferry Review*.

Kristin Hatch was the recipient two Hopwood Awards in Short Fiction from the University of Michigan, and later received an MFA from the Iowa Writers' Workshop. Her poems have appeared, or are forthcoming in *Can We Have Our Ball Back?, Dispatch Detroit*, and *The Madison Review*.

Anne Lendon Heide has a degree in film from the University of Wisconsin at Milwaukee and is currently working on an MA in Creative Writing at the University of Colorado at Boulder. Her work has appeared or is forthcoming in *LVNG, Curbside Review, Small Town, Diner, 26*, and *Indefinite Space*.

Jeanette Karhi holds an MFA from the Iowa Writers' Workshop. Her poetry has been published in *Poetry International, MARGIE, Washington Square, River Styx* and is forthcoming in *Stand*. www.jeannettekarhi.com

Erin Keane is the author of *The Gravity Soundtrack*, a full-length collection of poems forthcoming from *WordFarm* in 2007, and *The One-Hit Wonders* (Snark Publishing), a chapbook of poems about and inspired by rock & roll. Her poems, essays, and reviews have appeared or are forthcoming in many magazines, including *Nimrod, Spoon River Poetry Review, Poems & Plays, New Southerner, Now & Then*, and *Louisville Magazine*. She directs the InKY Reading Series in Louisville, KY.

Megan Kaminski teaches writing and yoga in Portland, OR. Her poems have recently appeared in *Can We Have Our Ball Back?*

L.S. Klatt has recent poems either appearing or forthcoming in *Field*, *Northwest Review*, *Bellingham Review*, *turnrow*, *Five Fingers Review*, *Notre Dame Review*, *Colorado Review*, and *Verse*.

David Koehn's poetry appears in a variety of publications such as *Rhino*, *VOLT*, *New England Review*, *NYQ*, and *ZYZZYVA*. Currently David lives outside San Francisco, CA and participates with a group of San Francisco Poets in a workshop called Thirteen Ways. Also, David recently started, and contributes to, an online poetics blog The Great American Pin-up partnered with Webdelsol at: http://greatamericanpinup.blogspot.com   web: http://davidkoehn.com

Jonathan Lethem is the author of nine novels, two books of short fiction and a collection of essays, as well as numerous other short works. He received the National Book Critics Circle Award for his novel, *Motherless Brooklyn*, and is a 2005 recipient of the MacArthur Fellowship. He has published in numerous journals, including *The New Yorker*, *Rolling Stone*, and *McSweeney's*.

J. Michael Martinez resides in Boulder, CO. He received his Bachelor of Arts from the University of Northern Colorado. He is winner of the *Five Fingers Review* Poetry Prize, 2006. He was the recipient of the 2005-2006 Thesis Completion Fellowship from George Mason University, where he completed his MFA in Poetry. He has been published in *Five Fingers Review*, *The Colorado Review*, *Crab Orchard Review*, *The Bitter Oleander, Practice* and others.

Kathleen McGookey's first book of poems, *Whatever Shines*, is available from White Pine Press. More of her translations of Godeau's work appear in *Chase Park*, *Connecticut Review*, *Denver Quarterly*, *The Interlochen Review*, *Mid-American Review*, *Natural Bridge*, *Rhino*, *Salt Hill*, and *Stand*. Her web site is www.kathleenmcgookey.com.

Phong Nguyen teaches writing at the University of Central Missouri. In '06-'07, his stories have appeared in *Iowa Review*, *Massachusetts Review*, *Florida Review*, *Southern Indiana Review*, *Portland Review*, *AGNI*, *Porcupine*, *Rosebud*, *Meridian*, *Inkwell*, *Confrontation*, *Beloit Fiction Journal*, and *Painted Bride Quarterly*. He is currently at work on a strange novel.

Russell Peagler was born and raised in Moncks Corner, South Carolina and currently resides in Tokyo, Japan. His influences include Robert Frank and Daido Moriyama. Upcoming shows include: "Tokyo in Five: the first train series," showing at the White House and Luftig, Bunkyoku, Tokyo; Selections from *Chasing the Bomb*, showing at the Eigakan, Tokyo; and, "Dialing Home" showing at Lander University in October. He holds a BA in Literature from Lander University, a Masters in International Relations, and studied Japanese at Jouchi Daigaku. Contact for inquires or sales at russellpeagler@yahoo.com.

Linda Plaisted, a GMU alumnus, is a painter, photographer and mixed media artist who has shown her work in galleries and museums throughout North America. She is the founder of Manymuses Studio and works in collaboration with fellow artists and artisans to create unique works of fine art and jewelry seen in exclusive galleries and boutiques around the world. www.manymuses.com

Eliza Rotterman lives in Eugene, Oregon where she is currently completing her MFA in poetry. From time to time she works part time on an organic vegetable farm. Next summer, she plans to take a bike trip with her partner from Vancouver, B.C. to Baja California.

Julie Marie Wade teaches Women's Studies at Carlow University. She holds an MA in English from Western Washington University and an MFA in Poetry from the University of Pittsburgh. She has recently received the Chicago Literary Award for Poetry, the *Gulf Coast* Nonfiction Prize, the Oscar Wilde Poetry Prize, the Literal Latte Nonfiction Prize, and a Pushchart Prize nomination. Her poem, "Law of Parsimony," is for Angie.

Fred Yannantuono was fired from Hallmark for writing meaningful greeting-card verse. He once ran twenty straight balls at pool. He finished 183rd (out of about 10,000) at the 1985 U.S. Open Crossword Puzzle Tournament. He won a yodeling contest in a German restaurant. Paul Newman once claimed to have known him for a long time. He hasn't been arrested in 17 months.

Maya Jewell Zeller grew up in rural Washington and Oregon. For three years she taught high school English and coached cross-country on the Olympic Peninsula, and is now an MFA candidate at Eastern Washington University in Spokane, where she serves as a poetry editor for *Willow Springs* and Editorial Assistant/Intern Coordinator for EWU Press. Her poems have appeared or are forthcoming in *Tidepools, Pontoon, Raven Chronicles online, Regarding Arts & Letters, Stringtown, Rattle, Ecotone, Slipstream,* and *Blue Earth Review.*

cream city review

30th anniversary issue
on memoir

~

Sven Birkerts
Robert Hill Long
Michael Martone
Thylias Moss
D. H. Tracy
Larissa Szporluk
Donald Platt
Jane Springer

~

single issue: $12
1-year subscription: $22
2-year subscription: $41

send check/M.O. to:

cream city review
UW-Milwaukee
English Department, Box 413
Milwaukee, WI 53201

So to Speak
a feminist journal of language and art

So to Speak has served as a space for feminist writing and art for twelve years. Published twice annually, the journal features work that addresses issues of significance to women's lives and movements for women's equality. We are particularly interested in pieces that explore issues of race, class, and sexuality in relation to gender.

Fiction   Poetry

George Mason University
4400 University Drive
MSD 2D6
Fairfax, VA 22030-4444
sts@gmu.edu
(no electronic submissions)

Visual Art   Nonfiction

2007 Annual Poetry and Non Fiction Contests

First Prize: $500 plus publication
Judges: TBA
Postmark Deadline: October 15, 2007

To be considered for our poetry contest, please submit 2-5 poems. Poems should appear on the page as you wish to see them published. For our non fiction contest please submit non-academic essays of 4,000 words maximum, including memoirs and vignettes. Manuscripts should be typed, and double-spaced, and pages numbered. To submit more than one essay or more than five poems, an additional $15 entry fee is required per entry. Entry fees should be sent via check or money order made out to *So to Speak*. Please include a cover letter indicating that your submission is a contest entry, how you heard about the contest, a brief bio, and a SASE. Mail contest entries to: *So to Speak*, GMU, 4400 University Dr., MS 2D6, Fairfax, VA 22030-4444.

Subscribe to *So to Speak*: only $12 for a one year subscription, $20 for two years.

For information about the contest, submission guidelines, and for subscription information, visit **www.gmu.edu/org/sts**.

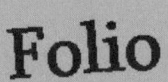

Folio

Folio: a literary journal
Department of Literature
American University
Washington, DC 20016

Please visit our website: www.foliojournal.org

santa clara review
celebrating 139 years

(because an even number just isn't artsy enough)

Help us celebrate by sending your best poetry, fiction, non-fiction or art to:

Santa Clara Review (Anniversary)
500 El Camino Real, #3212
Santa Clara, CA 95053-3212

Or submit online at:
www.santaclarareview.com/submit

A LITERARY MAGAZINE THAT BRIDGES THE GAP BETWEEN SERIOUS ART AND POP CULTURE.

Barrelhouse

FICTION.
POETRY.
POP FLOTSAM.
CULTURAL JETSAM.

WWW.BARRELHOUSEMAG.COM

PHOEBE
a journal of literature and art
Become a *Phoebe Friend*

Have Your Name listed here with other *Phoebe Friend* donators
and
receive a complimentary two-year subscription!

Support: poetry ⌘   fiction ⌘   interviews ⌘   art

Your donation of $50 or above will entitle you to a complimentary two-year subscription and to having your name printed in the Fall 2007 issue of the journal as a *Phoebe Friend*.

Donations received will go to the support of the journal, printing costs, and advertising. Anonymous donations are welcome. All donations are tax-deductible.

Donation checks should be made payable to: GMU Foundation with "Phoebe/University Life" in the memo line.

To subscribe, submit or **donate** send name and address with a check or money order to:

Phoebe
George Mason University
MSN 2D6, 4400 University Drive
Fairfax VA 22030

http://www.gmu.edu/pubs/phoebe

"Definitely a journal to keep watching."   —*NewPages.com*

PHOEBE
A Journal of Literature and Art

Since 1971, *Phoebe* has been devoted to publishing outstanding fiction, poetry, and art. While regularly featuring contributions from major contemporary authors, *Phoebe* prides itself on discovering original work from new voices. Past contributors include:

Joyce Carol Oates, Edward P. Jones, Maxine Kumin, John Gardner, Fanny Howe, Peter Streckfus, Carolyn Forché, Stephen Dobyns, Denise Levertov, Stuart Dybek, Rosmarie Waldrop, Russell Edson, Yusef Komunyakaa, William Stafford, and more.

Phoebe's annual contests in fiction and poetry offer $1000 and publication. Recent judges include Anne Carson, Tom Franklin, Robert Creeley, and Richard Ford. Entries due on Dec. 1. Complete guidelines available at website.

Phoebe
George Mason University
MSN 2D6 / 4400 University Drive
Fairfax, VA 22030
www.gmu.edu/pubs/phoebe